Celebrate with Crafts

*Projects for
Every Occasion*

 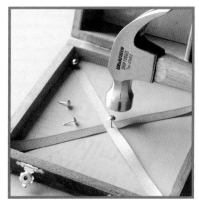 

CREATIVE
HOME
ARTS
—CLUB—

Minnetonka, Minnesota

Celebrate with Crafts

Projects for Every Occasion

Printed in 2008.

Tom Carpenter
Creative Director

Jen Weaverling
Production Editor

Kate Opseth
Design and Production

Phil Aarrestad
Principal Photographer

Maggie Stopera, Susan Telleen
Craft Stylists

Contributing Writers
Sue Banker
Zoe Graul
Margaret Hanson-Maddox
Eileen Hull
Chris Malone
Lorine Mason
Cheryl Natt
Cheryl Nelson
Monica Tikkanen

Special thanks to: Mike Billstein, Terry Casey, Janice Cauley, John Keenan, Heather Koshiol and Bill Stephani.

1 2 3 4 5 6 7 8 9 10 /10 09 08 07
© 2008 Creative Home Arts Club
ISBN: 978-1-58159-327-3

Creative Home Arts Club
12301 Whitewater Drive
Minnetonka, MN 55343
www.creativehomeartsclub.com

Contents

Celebrate with Crafts
Introduction

4

There are indeed two ways to celebrate with crafts.

The first and most obvious way is to put your finished creations to good use. Maybe that purpose is to beautify your home, make an occasion more special or even happier, or enrich someone's life with a special handmade gift that was made with love and care.

The second way to celebrate with crafts involves the creative process itself. Simply put, crafting is fun. It's a release, it's an escape, it's challenging, it's relaxing … this list could go on and on, but the idea is crystal clear: It's perfectly fine to craft just for the sheer joy of it.

Those two ideas formed the basis for *Celebrate with Crafts.* Our pastime truly does offer double rewards! But sometimes you need a few ideas and instructions along the way, to help you get started and then bring the project to beautiful completion. That's where these pages come in.

Here are dozens upon dozens of craft ideas to fulfill your every whim and fancy … an entire year's worth of creations. When you look at a calendar, every season offers opportunities for creating a variety of delightful projects. So we take you from beginning to end … from New Year's and Valentine's Day through Easter and the Fourth of July, on to Thanksgiving, Halloween and Christmas.

But what makes this book extra fun is that you get project plans for the holidays and occasions you might not otherwise think of or craft for. St. Patrick's Day, Cinco de Mayo, Memorial Day and Grandparents Day all get plenty of attention here, as do Mother's Day and Father's Day.

To make sure your crafting journey is a rewarding one, we've added a variety of features to each project to assure your crafting success. A big color photograph shows every finished creation so you know exactly what you're working toward. Clear materials and tools lists help you gather what you need to get to work. Helpful patterns make you efficient. And step-by-step instructions—anchored by photographs of key steps in the process—guide you to certain success.

Yes, it's time to *Celebrate with Crafts.* These projects take you there and assure your success. And remember: Have fun doing the creating, and then enjoying the rewards!

new years
Confetti Place Mats

Materials

- ½ yard each: red and black medium-weight fabric, 60" wide
- ⅛ yard cotton print fabric (for appliqués and napkins)
- ⅛ yard lightweight clear vinyl
- Thread: black, silver
- 20" of ¼" flat braid trim
- Straight pins
- Scrap of tissue paper
- Masking tape

Tools

- Sewing machine
- Iron
- See-through ruler
- Marking pencil

Create these fun-filled place mats with hat and noisemaker appliqués—and a balloon filled with confetti. Make coordinating napkins for an even more festive look.

COST: $10.00

TIME: 2 hours

- Enlarge and cut out patterns (see page 145).
- Pre-wash and iron fabrics.
- See photos for details and placement.

1 Cut pieces. Trace and cut two hats and two noisemakers from print fabric. From both the black and red fabric, measure and cut two 14" x 18" rectangles. For napkins, cut two 18" squares from print fabric.

2 Attach appliqués. Pin hat at an angle in lower right corner on right side of black fabric. Pin noisemaker at angle in upper right corner. Keep designs 1" from edge of fabric. Use black thread to baste stitch appliqués in place. Zigzag stitch around each appliqué. Note: Contrast thread was used to show stitching in photo. Use silver thread to zigzag stitch a "pom-pom" at top of hat, using three intersecting lines. In the same way, zigzag stitch five "streamers"

coming out end of noisemaker. Mark random placement of "confetti" with pins. Zigzag stitch ½" long pieces of "confetti."

3 Sew balloon. Cut a 4½" square of vinyl. Place it on back of black fabric in upper left corner, 1"

from fabric edges. Pin vinyl close to edges. Trace balloon on right side of fabric at an angle 1½" from fabric edges. Note: Place a piece of tissue paper under vinyl when stitching. Baste stitch around traced balloon. To cut away the fabric inside of balloon, use a pin to pick up the fabric and trim close to the inside of the stitching. On wrong side, tear away tissue paper and trim vinyl ½" from stitching.

4 Sew place mat. Pin a red and black rectangle with right sides together. Sew a ½" seam around

the outside edges, leaving 3" open for turning. Trim corners at an angle. Turn right side out and push out corners. Press with iron.

5 Attach braid. Start at bottom of balloon and place braid around outside edges, covering stitching. Use small pieces of masking tape to hold braid in place. Tape the "tail" of balloon in place, looping it down the side of place mat. Note: To keep trim from raveling, wrap tape around ends until ready to sew. Baste stitch 1" away from center of trim, continuing around, over the cut edge and to end of "tail" removing tape ahead of stitching. Zigzag stitch over the end of "tail." Knot thread on back.

6 Finish. Make a paper funnel to insert confetti into balloon. Make sure that the confetti is out of the way and stitch the trim over opening, as above. Press a ½" seam allowance to the inside along opening of place mat. Pin in place and topstitch around outside edge of place mat. Iron place mat but do not press over vinyl area. Note: Apply Scotchgard if you like.

Party Hat
Centerpieces

Materials

- Party-theme paper: garland, noisemakers, small hats, clocks
- Blue poster board
- Adhesive clock faces
- Tape
- Metallic gold and silver self-adhesive letters and words
- Metallic curling ribbon in a variety of colors

Tools

- Hot-glue gun and glue sticks
- Scissors

An oversized party hat dresses a table in style to ring in the New Year. Scrapbooking and clock-making materials provide the winning combination.

COST: $21.00

TIME: 1½ hours

- See photos for details and placement.

1 Make hat. Starting at one corner of the poster board, loosely roll a cone in the shape of an oversized party hat. Place on head to determine size. Glue together along overlapping edge of poster board. Tape the inside seam for added security.

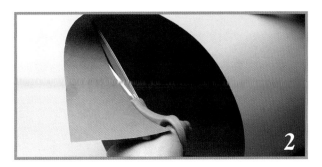

2 Trim hat. Use scissors to trim the bottom edge even so the hat sits flat.

3 Decorate hat. Peel off the backing papers and adhere the clock face to the hat front. Glue one clock hand to point to the 12 on the clock face. Apply sticker letters and numbers, placing them at a consistent angle. Include the year and words like "tick-tock," "Happy New Year," and "celebrate." Carefully press the letters to the poster board so you don't crease it.

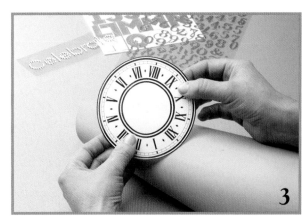

4 Attach ribbons. Cut several 18" lengths of curling ribbon. Curl the ribbon by scraping with edge of scissors. Tape all of the ribbons together in the center. Tuck the taped portion of the ribbons in the hole at the top of the hat to appear as if streamers are coming out the top.

5 Finish. Place the hat in the center of time-theme scrapbook papers. Surround the hat with items, such as metallic garland, clocks, curling ribbon, purchased hats, and noisemakers.

Beaded Napkin Holder
& Wine Glass Decorations

Materials

- Bracelet memory wire
- Two 4" pieces of 22-gauge silver plastic-coated wire
- Black word bead
- 75 assorted 3mm to 8mm glass beads: Silver, red, white, black
- Beverage I.D. wire hoop

Tools

- Wire cutter
- Needle-nose pliers
- Toothpick

String silver and glass beads on wire circles to make beautiful table accessories. Use a different word bead for each wine glass so guests can identify their glasses.

COST: $6.00 for one set

TIME: 45 minutes for one set

- See photos for details and placement.

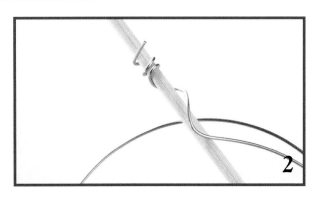

Wine Glass ID:

1 Attach beads. String beads onto wire hoop in random order until only ⅜" of wire is bare. Join wire ends together.

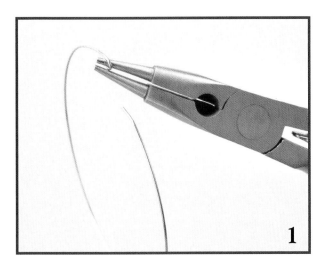

2 Attach dangle. Cut 4" length of silver wire. Wrap wire around toothpick to make two small loops to hold beads. String beads onto wire in random order until only ⅜" of wire is left. Wrap end of wire once around center of beaded hoop. Wrap wire end around toothpick several times to make two small loops.

Napkin Holder:

1 Prepare wire. Cut piece from memory wire that includes two complete circles. Use tip of pliers to bend a small loop at one end of wire to keep beads from falling off.

2 Attach beads. String beads onto wire in a random order until only ⅜" of wire is left. Wrap wire around toothpick to make two small loops to hold beads.

Happy New Year
Garland

Materials

- 6-inch wood numbers for year
- Metallic acrylic paints: turquoise, copper, pink, purple, silver
- Acrylic paints: green, orange, red, royal blue
- 72" of multi-color feather boa
- Two coordinating jewel bauble ornaments
- Brass cup hooks
- Disposable container for paint

Tools

- Paintbrushes: flat and fan

Drape a feathery boa to celebrate the New Year. The artsy wood letters are accented with crosshatch paint strokes and bead dangles to complete the festive garland.

COST: $21.00

TIME: 1½ hours

- Let paint dry thoroughly after each application.
- See photos for details and placement.

1 Paint base coat. Use a flat paintbrush to paint the wood numerals in the following colors: turquoise, copper, pink, and purple.

2 Paint highlights. Use the fan brush and very little silver paint to randomly paint crosshatch (X strokes) over each numeral, allowing the base color to show through.

3 Paint top coat. Use the same crosshatch technique to paint the numerals with a top coat of paint in the following colors: green, orange, red, and royal blue.

4 Attach screws. Screw a cup hook into the top of each painted numeral, facing the hook to the back.

5 Attach ornaments. Hook an ornament on each end loop of the feather boa. Note: Make the boa shorter by cutting the string and tying the end into a loop.

6 Finish. Hang the boa at two points as you like. Hook on the numerals in order, centering them on the boa.

Embellished
Place Mat & Napkin

Materials

- Ready-made red fabric place mat and napkin
- Black pearl cotton thread, size 5
- Scraps of three black and white geometric print fabrics
- Paper-backed iron-on adhesive

Tools

- Air-erasable pen
- Ruler
- Embroidery needle
- Pins
- Thimble (optional)
- Iron
- Scissors

Create a fun yet sophisticated New Year's Eve table setting using geometric shapes and a red, black, and white color scheme.

COST: $21.00 for hat only

TIME: 1½ hours

- Enlarge and cut out patterns. (see page 146)
- Use one strand of pearl cotton for all embroidery.
- See photos for details and placement.

Napkin:

1 Hemmed napkin. If napkin already has a hemmed finish, use pearl cotton thread to add large running stitches on top of machine stitching line.

2 Serged napkin. If napkin has a serged edge in a matching or desirable color, use pearl cotton thread to add large running stitches ¼" in from the edge. Note: If napkin has a serged edge in an unwanted color, cut it off. To hem napkin, fold ¼" to wrong side and press down. Press ¼" to wrong side again and press down. Sew in place close to inside folded edge. Use pearl cotton thread to add large running stitches on top of machine stitching line.

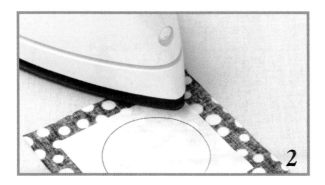

Place Mat:

1 Stitch design. Transfer scroll pattern to right side of place mat with air-erasable pen. Embroider a chain stitch along pattern line.

2 Fuse circles. Trace circle patterns onto paper side of iron-on adhesive, leaving space between each circle. Cut apart, leaving a square around each circle. Follow manufacturer's directions to apply a circle to wrong side of each fabric scrap. Cut out circles and remove paper backing. Place circles along scroll lines on front of place mat and fuse in place with iron.

3 Stitch circles. Blanket stitch around edges of each circle with pearl cotton thread.

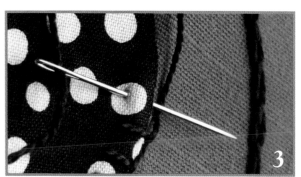

15

valentine's day
Sweet Tooth Bouquet

16

Materials

- Floral bush
- Baby's breath floral spray
- Assorted foil-wrapped candies
- 2 sheets pink tissue paper
- 5 1/2" x 9" pink polka-dot paper
- 2 "Valentine" 1 1/2" squares of paper
- 2 1/2 yards of 1" wide sheer fuchsia ribbon
- 12" of 1/4" sheer fuchsia ribbon
- Floral wire
- Paper glue stick

Tools

- Wire cutter
- Glue gun and glue sticks
- 1/4" circle punch
- Decorative-edge scissors: mini scallop
- Scissors

Combine a bouquet of pretty flowers with chocolate treats hidden amongst the petals. Your sweetheart will be impressed when presented with not just one but two of her favorites.

COST: $12.00

TIME: 1 hour

- See photos for details and placement.

1 Make bouquet. Separate the baby's breath floral stems and cut apart. Glue individual stems between flowers in floral bush. Separate the petals of each flower and glue a candy into the center using the glue gun.

2 Wrap bouquet. Wrap tissue paper around the bouquet and tie a two-loop bow with the 1" ribbon. Wrap the ribbon ends around the stems of the flowers and tissue paper down to the end of stems, crossing the ribbons over each other. Repeat back up the stems of the flowers. Tie the two ribbon ends together in a knot and trim ends at a slant. Add a drop of glue to hold ribbon ties in place.

3 Make gift card. Fold the polka-dot paper rectangle in half to measure 2¾" x 9". Use decorative scissor to trim along the unfolded edges. Use the glue stick to glue edges together. Fold the smaller rectangle into thirds, each measuring 2¾" x 3". Fold the center section in half. Glue one "Valentine" square over center fold and other one on front section of card. Punch a hole in back section of card near top of fold. Insert ¼" wide ribbon into hole. Tie ribbon in a knot around one stem of bouquet.

Pick Your Hors-d'Oeuvres

Materials

- 1 package turkey lacers
- 1 metal skewer
- Assorted beads and spacers
- Superglue

Tools

- Round needle-nose pliers (for jewelry)

Win your sweetheart's heart with these lovely heart hors-d'oeuvre picks. The picks are easy and quick to make and add a touch of style to your dinner party tray of appetizers.

COST: $10.00

TIME: 45 minutes

- For the "pick," buy a package of turkey lacers from the grocery store. Make sure it will fit into the holes of the beads and spacers.
- Use superglue that has a small nozzle applicator.
- See photos for details and placement.

1 Preparation. Select your color and design scheme in heart beads and spacers to match the holiday.

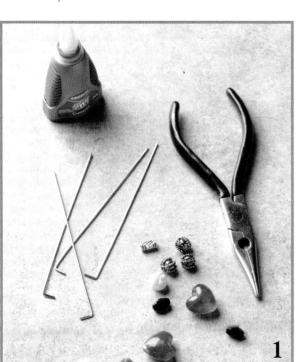

2 Make loops. Depending on the style of the turkey lacer, you may need to use the needle-nose pliers make a loop on the top end. Make a set of six picks.

3 Add beads. Arrange the beads and spacers on the turkey lacer in the order that you like, leaving 1" open at the sharp end of the pick. Turn the pick upside down. Separate each bead and place a dab of superglue between each one. Be careful to keep all the beads up tight on the shaft of the pick. When dry, wash and store.

19

Hearts of Gold Wreath

Materials

- 9" raft foam heart wreath
- 2 pounds red and gold flat glass marbles
- 6 yards of 7/8" red and white ribbon
- Straight pins

Tools

- Glue gun and glue sticks

Show your commitment to 'Love' with this gem covered wreath. The warmth of the gold combined with the fire-hot red gems make this wreath almost too hot to handle.

COST: $15.00

TIME: 1½ hours

- See photos for details and placement.

1 Wrap heart. Starting at the bottom point of the heart, wrap the wreath with ribbon. Use straight pins to hold ribbon in place around curves. Pin folds in ribbon if necessary to remove bulk.

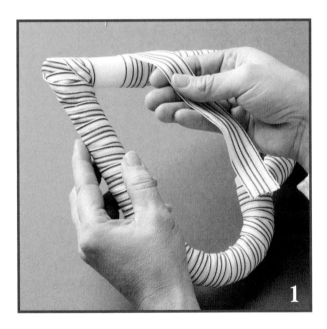

3 Tie hanger. Cut an 18" length of ribbon and tie the two ends together in an overhand knot. Lay the heart on top of the loop of ribbon and bring tied end of the ribbon through the opposite end of loop.

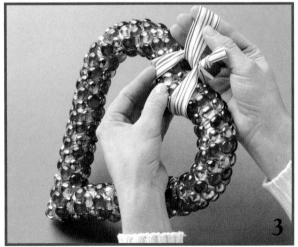

2 Add stones. Glue marbles to heart, alternating rows of red and gold. Note: Glue stones to the front and sides of heart where they will be seen. Leave back bare so wreath will lie flat on wall and to lessen weight.

4 Make bow. Make a multi-looped bow with six 4" loops and 6" tails. Glue bow to the top front of the wreath.

Hearts-o-Mine Garland

Materials

- 2 heart garlands
- 6 wooden hearts, 2½" wide
- Acrylic craft paints: red, pink
- Large heart stamp
- Small single flower stamp
- Stamp pads: red, silver
- Buttons or heart-shaped hard candies
- 50" of 20-gauge wire

Tools

- Drill and ⅛" bit
- Small paintbrush
- Awl
- Glue gun and glue sticks
- Wire cutter
- Needle-nose pliers

Create a decoration for the table, wall, or over a door with stamped wooden hearts attached to purchased garlands. Buttons or candies are added for dimension.

COST: $9.00 (not including stamps and stamp pad)

TIME: 1½ hours

- Let paint dry thoroughly after each application.
- See photos for details and placement.

1 Paint and stamp hearts. Drill hole in center top of wooden hearts. Paint two hearts pink and four hearts red. Using the flower stamp and red stamp pad, randomly stamp flowers and hearts on the pink hearts. Using the same stamp and silver stamp pad, stamp flowers and hearts on the red hearts.

2 Decorate hearts. Glue heart-shaped buttons or hard candy on the hearts. Note: Shanks can usually be removed with pliers.

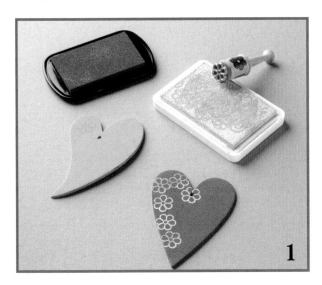

3 Make hangers. Cut six lengths of wire 8" long. Wrap end of wire around the end of an awl or similar size tool to make 3 small loops. Insert a wire into hole in each heart from front to back.

4 Finish. Twist ends of two heart garlands together. Make a loop at each end for hanging. Secure hearts on garland by wrapping wire around garland.

23

Beaded Box

Materials

- 4½" wooden or papier-mâché heart-shaped box
- Medium-weight satin fabric
- 1 strand black iridescent seed beads
- 1 strand red seed beads
- Measuring tape
- Sewing thread: black, red
- 5" square of medium-weight batting
- 14" of fringe trim (width of side of box top)
- Fabric glue

Tools

- Paper, pencil or pen
- Light chalk pencil or quilter's silver pencil
- Scissors
- 7" embroidery hoop
- Sewing needle
- Pen
- 8 spring-type clothespins

Turn a wooden or papier-mâché heart-shaped box into an elegant gift or jewelry box, by adding iridescent beads to an elegant-rich fabric to cover the box top. If you want to spend more time on the project, add individual seed beads randomly.

COST: $9.00

TIME: 2 hours

- Enlarge pattern to fit within edge of top of box (see page 147) and cut out.
- See photos for details and placement.

1 Trace and cut fabric cover. For cutting line, add the depth of the box side plus ⅛" around the outside of the pattern. Cut out pattern. Cut a 9" square of fabric. With chalk pencil, center and trace the top of heart box on the right side of fabric square. With pen, trace around the box top on batting and cut out for later use.

2 Attach black beads. Use the chalk pencil to draw a line ¼" inside the heart for the first design. Place fabric in embroidery hoop. Do not stretch. Fold the string of black beads in half. Use two strands of black thread and start at the top of the heart. Insert the needle from the back, coming up on the design line next to the two strings of beads. Note: Beads should be on the inside of line. Go over the strings of beads and insert needle back into the fabric. Continue this way around the heart shape. Remove extra beads from bead strand and thread ends through needle. Bring needle through fabric to back and knot threads securely.

3 Attach red beads. Trace center design on fabric. Use two strands of red thread and one string of red beads, to stitch beads down in same way as in Step 2. Remove fabric from embroidery hoop. Use paper pattern from Step 1 to trace and cut fabric for top of box.

4 Finish. Glue batting to top of box. Center fabric, stretching slightly, and hold in place with clothespins. Glue at top, bottom, and sides and then in between. Trim away any extending fabric. Cut fringe trim to fit around top of box plus ¼". Starting at top, glue end of fringe in place and hold until secure. Continue gluing around the box, overlapping ends at top. Note: White glue will disappear when dry.

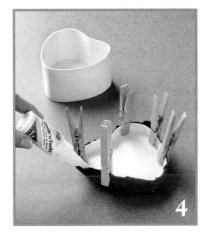

Rose Blossom Hanging Heart

Materials

- 5" wide wooden heart shape
- Spray or acrylic paint to match color of roses
- 10" of 24-gauge wire
- 1 yard of green ¼" velvet ribbon
- 33 assorted sizes of artificial mini-rose blossoms

Tools

- Drill and ⅛" drill bit
- Wire cutter
- Paintbrush (if using acrylics)
- Glue gun and glue sticks
- Toothpicks
- Scissors

A cluster of artificial mini-roses glued to a wooden heart shape makes a delicate hanging for Valentine's Day or a nice gift for someone special. Dried roses may be used but are fragile. You may choose artificial ones that resemble dried roses for durability.

COST: $26.00

TIME: ½ hour

- See photos for details and placement.

1 Prepare heart. Drill two holes at the top center of the wooden heart. Paint heart pink. Let dry. Insert wire halfway through holes. Twist wire together close to heart.

3 Attach roses. Cut roses close to the blossom. Use glue gun to apply glue to the back of the rose and press on wooden heart, starting at top center to cover the base of the wire and holes. Hold until secure. Glue hearts first around the outside edge.

2 Attach border ribbon. Cut ribbon to fit around the outside of the wooden heart. Starting at the top center of the heart, glue ribbon along edge using glue gun. Keep ribbon edge even with back edge of heart. Cut ribbon at center top.

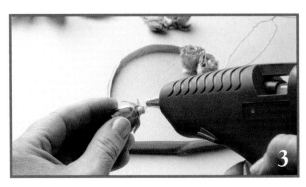

Keep smaller roses to fill in spaces Note: Use a toothpick to separate petals and hold in place while gluing roses into small areas.

4 Finish. Tie ribbon in a bow and cut ends at a slant. Glue bow to the base of the hanging wire.

Materials

- One sheet of lime green/white polka-dot felt
- 14" square of black felt
- Embroidery floss: lime green, bright pink
- 1¾ yard of 1½" light lime green grosgrain ribbon
- Tracing paper
- Straight pins

Tools

- Pencil
- Sewing needle
- Scissors

Bring the fun and festivity of St. Patrick's Day to your table. Polka-dot felt and easy-to-do stitches add whimsy.

COST: $16.00

TIME: 2 hours

- Enlarge patterns (see page 147) and cut out.
- Use three strands of embroidery floss for all stitching.
- See photos for details and placement.
- See page 144 for stitches.

1 Make patterns. Trace the large heart, six small hearts, and the two stem patterns onto tracing paper. Cut out the patterns.

2 Cut out clovers. Trace six large hearts and two stems onto polka-dot felt. Cut out hearts and stems.

3 Attach clovers. Pin three hearts for each of the two large clovers to the black felt background. Pin a stem below each clover. Thread the needle with pink floss and knot one end. Insert needle into back of the mat and push the needle through next to one of the hearts. Work blanket stitches around the edge of all clovers pieces.

4 Outline small clovers. Pin the small hearts and small stems to the black felt in same way as

large clovers, using the photo for placement. Thread the needle with a long length of lime floss. Use running stitches to outline the clover shape. Remove the patterns.

5 Attach border. Pin the ribbon to the felt edge, folding it over at the corners. Use pink floss and long running stitches to secure the ribbon to the edge of the table topper. Secure the folded corners of the ribbon by taking a small stitch with pink floss in the center of each corner. Knot and cut thread on back of mat.

"All That Glitters" Shamrock Garland

Materials

- ⅛ yard of shamrock-print fabric
- 5 wooden 5" shamrock shapes
- White base paint
- 60" of string
- Acrylic paints: medium green, pastel green
- 3-D gold glitter paint
- 1" masking tape

Tools

- Drill and ⅛" bit
- Paintbrushes: ½", ¾"
- Natural sea sponge
- Scissors

Use easy freehand painted designs and 3-D glitter paint to make this contemporary shamrock garland. Place it on your mantle, wall, door, or above the door.

COST: $8.00

TIME: 1 hour

- Allow paint to dry thoroughly after each application.
- The 3-D glitter paint will take longer to dry completely.
- See photos for details and placement.

1 Drill shamrocks. Drill holes at outside edges of shamrocks where you want them to join. Note: Some shamrocks can be made to hang upside down by putting the holes toward the bottom of outside leaf.

2 Paint shamrocks. Paint each shamrock with a white base coat. Use larger brush to paint shamrocks medium green. Sponge shamrocks with pastel green.

3 Paint designs. Use the following ideas for painting the shamrocks or come up with your own ideas:
A) Use green paint and smaller paintbrush to make circles on shamrock. Use 3-D glitter paint to outline the circles.
B) Use 3-D glitter paint to outline the shamrock.
C) To create stripes, cover the shamrock with strips of tape ¾" apart. Press down all edges well. Paint two coats with green paint. Remove tape.
D) Make a plaid design by placing strips of tape going in opposite directions.

4 Hang shamrocks. Cut six 10" lengths of string. Insert string into two adjoining holes, leaving about 2" between shamrocks. Tie string in a knot and clip ends. Cut slits into selvage of fabric 1" apart and tear strips of fabric. Cut 8" lengths and tie strips around string to cover it. For hanging, make loop on the end of two strings. Tie them into the holes of the outside shamrocks. Tie several fabric ties around the strings.

Celtic Card

Materials

- 5½" x 8½" gold card stock
- Light green Celtic print paper
- 3 mini craft sticks
- 4" x 4" green paper
- Glue
- "Happy St. Patrick's Day" stamp
- Stamp pads: green, brown
- Foam dots
- 8" of ¼" gold ribbon

Tools

- Paper heart punch
- Scissors

Why "knot" send St. Patrick's Day greetings this year to friends and family? Everyone enjoys wishes of good luck!

COST: 10 cards for $12.00

TIME: 1 hour

- Trace and cut out stem pattern.

1 Make card. Fold gold card stock in half lengthwise to measure 4¼" x 5½". Cut a 4" x 5¼" piece from light green paper. Glue on card.

2 Add strip. Tear a strip of gold paper about 2½" x 5". Rub brown ink on torn edges to distress.

3 Make shamrock. From light green paper, punch six hearts. Cut a stem shape. Fold hearts in half down the middle and rub brown ink on edges. Arrange two hearts for each of three leaves to form shamrock shape. Cut a stem.

4 Stamp message. Stamp "Happy St. Patrick's Day" on craft sticks using green ink pad. Rub brown ink on edges of sticks.

5 Assemble. Glue gold torn strip to front of card. Glue shamrock on one end of gold strip. Tie gold ribbon in a knot around center of strip. Glue craft sticks on other end of strip.

Pot of Gold Wreath

Materials

- 8" craft foam wreath
- 8 yards of ⅞" green/gold sheer ribbon
- 2 lbs. green flat glass marbles
- 1 lb. gold mini flat glass marbles
- 1½" terra-cotta pot
- Metallic gold spray paint
- Straight pins

Tools

- Glue gun and glue sticks
- Scissors

Celebrate your belief in the "Luck of the Irish" by displaying a wreath filled with shiny glass marbles to welcome your guests.

COST: $18.00

TIME: 1½ hours

- See photos for details and placement.

1 Wrap ribbon. Wrap wreath with four yards of ribbon, using straight pins to hold ribbon in place.

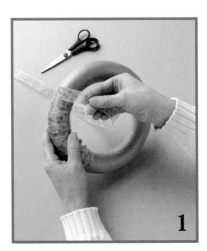

2 Glue marbles. Glue green gems to wreath, leaving a 4" section open on bottom. Do not glue marbles to the back of wreath to eliminate bulk and weight.

3 Paint pot. Spray paint the pot gold. Let dry. Glue pot to wreath.

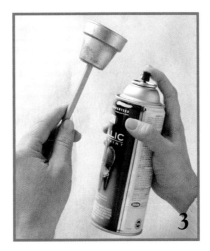

4 Glue marbles. Glue gold marbles into the open space overlapping the green marbles to appear to be spilling from the pot.

5 Make hanger. Cut an 18" length of ribbon and tie the two ends together in an overhand knot. Lay the wreath on the loop of ribbon and bring one end of the ribbon through the opposite end of the loop.

6 Make bow. Use 2½ yards of ribbon to make a multi-looped bow with twelve 4" loops and 6" tails. Measure 14" of ribbon and fold the ribbon back on itself. Measure 8" of ribbon and fold in opposite direction. Continue measuring and folding 8" loops of ribbon until you have four folds on each side. Cut a 6" length of ribbon to tie around the center of ribbon folds. For the ties, cut two 6" lengths of ribbon and glue them under the knot. Trim ends of ribbons at a slant. Glue bow to top of wreath.

Rub-on Instant
Holiday Decoration

Materials

- Pre-stamped rub-on decal
- Clay pot, planter, or cup
- Acrylic spray or lacquer spray
- White spray paint (or color of choice)

Tools

- Craft stick (in rub-on decal package)
- Scissors

Rub-on decals are a perfect way to create a special gift for any occasion. Decorate a planter, vase, or cup for Easter with simple decal patterns. Use acrylic spray to protect the decal from water and scratching.

COST: $10.00

TIME: 30 minutes

- Let paint dry thoroughly after each application.
- See photos for details and placement.

1 Paint pot. Clean pot with a wet cloth to remove any dirt or dust particles. Let dry thoroughly. Spray-paint pot white. Let paint dry several hours before attaching the rub-on decal.

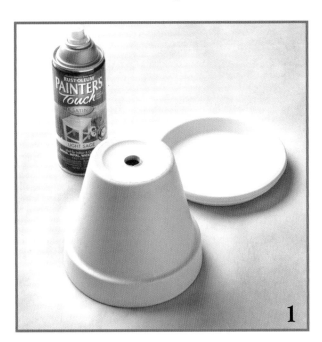

2 Attach decal. Follow the instructions on the decal. Cut the outside edge of the decal to the size needed for the planter. Remove protective backing.

Position rub-on decal right side up on planter. Cover with transfer paper and rub slightly with rub-on craft stick. Lift the transfer paper carefully to ensure decal is in place. If not, reposition decal, and rub on again until complete decal is in place. Repeat until all desired decals are in place on the pot.

3 Finish. Spray with acrylic spray. Spray a second coat to ensure that the shininess is the same on all areas. Fill pot with potting soil. Insert a living plant or bulbs.

Wall Hanging Quilt

Materials

- Embroidery floss (use colors for the season)
- ½ yard of fabric (of each): yellow (inside border) blue/yellow print (outside border) blue (binding)
- Pre-stamped quilt block
- ½ yard of fabric for backing of quilt
- 18" x 24" quilt batting
- Matching sewing thread
- Wooden dowel (for hanging)

Tools

- Embroidery hoop
- Embroidery needle
- Sewing needle
- Rotary cutter and mat
- Sewing machine
- Scissors

You may create this quilt for different holidays, varying the decoration depending upon the season.

COST: $12.00

TIME: 2 hours

- Use ¼" seam allowance unless otherwise indicated.
- Join pieces with right sides together.
- See photos for details and placement.
- See page 144 for stitches.

1 Stitch quilt block. Place fabric block in a large embroidery hoop and stretch the fabric tightly. Follow instructions for stitching the pre-stamped quilt block with two to three strands of embroidery floss. Use the appropriate backstitch, French knot, or cross-stitch according to the stamped pattern. When stitching is complete, wash the remaining stamped pattern from the fabric. Dry, press, and trim fabric to desired size for the center square using a rotary cutter and cutting mat. Leave ¼" seam allowance on outside edge.

1

2 Cut and sew borders. Cut the border fabrics into 2" (inside) and 3" (outside) strips using a rotary cutter and cutting mat. Sew the 2" strip to the top and bottom of the stitched block. Press to outside edge. Sew right and left sides of the 2" fabric strip to the stitched block and press to the outside. Trim outside edges of border with rotary cutter as needed to square. Repeat these steps to sew the 3" outside border to the inside border.

3 Assemble and stitch quilt. Press all remaining fabric to remove wrinkles. Layer the quilt back fabric right side down, and then the batting and stitched block right side up. Pin quilt through all layers starting between the first border and stitched fabric block. Stitch "in the ditch" (on top of stitched seams). Smooth all layers, pin, and stitch "in the ditch" between the second and first border. Smooth all layers again.

4 Cut and sew binding. Cut the binding into two or three strips as needed for quilt. To join strips together, sew short ends together. Press seams to one side. Fold binding in half lengthwise with wrong sides together and press to create a 1½" binding. To begin, fold the starting corner over to give the piece a finished look. Starting at the center bottom of the stitched block, with raw edges matching, pin and sew binding through all layers. At the corners, lift needle out of fabric. Fold binding at a 45-degree angle and then fold the binding down over the 45-degree angle and replace needle in same spot and continue sewing through all layers, folding at each corner until you reach the starting point. At starting point, overlap fabric by an inch or two and trim remaining binding off. Sew to end of trimmed binding. Press binding toward outside edge, fold in half over the edge, and pin to backing. Hand stitch to back of quilt using a binding stitch, needle, and matching thread. Be sure to fold corners on back side of binding at a 45-degree angle when stitching to maintain a square look on front and back of the quilt.

4

5 Finish. For hanging, attach a small wooden dowel along top of quilt using a needle and thread.

For the Birds

Materials

- *12" square of tulle net: blue, white*
- *12" of 1" blue striped ribbon*
- *Bird in a nest*
- *Small plastic margarine containers*
- *Plastic wrap*
- *Rubber band*

Tools

- *Mixing bowl*
- *Large spoon*
- *Hotglue gun and glue sticks*
- *Saucepan*
- *Stove*
- *Freezer*

Your favorite nature lover will love this tasty treat that will bring in the birds. And while you're at it, make some for your backyard, too!

BIRD SUET RECIPE

1 cup lard
1 cup crunchy peanut butter
2 cups "quick cook" or regular oats
2 cups cornmeal
1 cup white flour

COST: Under $10.00

TIME: 30 minutes

- Yield: Multiple suet cakes, depending on size.
- See photos for details and placement.

1 Make suet. Melt the lard and peanut butter in a saucepan over low heat. In a mixing bowl, mix the oats, cornmeal, and flour together. Stir in the melted lard and peanut butter.

2 Freeze suet. Fill small plastic margarine containers (or something of similar size) and freeze. Remove from the container.

Wrap in plastic wrap and store in the freezer until ready to serve to the birds outside.

3 Gift wrap. To dress up your suet cake for gift giving, cut two 12" squares of each color of tulle. Layer tulle squares on top of each other. Place suet in center of tulle. Gather the tulle together at the top and wind a rubber band around it. Tie ribbon in a bow around band. Cut ends at a slant. Attach bird in a nest with hotglue gun. Cut away any excess tulle. Be sure to include a copy of the Bird Suet recipe with your gift.

Imagine

- *Tie up your gift with raffia instead of ribbon.*
- *Spread suet mixture into a cake pan and cut into square blocks after freezing.*
- *Serve suet in a convenient store-bought suet cage.*
- *Serve suet cakes in plastic mesh onion or citrus bags.*
- *Make a simple suet feeder out of a milk carton. Spoon the mixture into the carton, freeze, let it cool, and then cut the sides or top out of the carton.*
- *Serve suet on a plate, in cat food or tuna cans, or on the ground.*

Tin Full of
Hydrangeas

Materials

- Purchased or computer-generated Easter greeting card
- Plain card stock (if a computer-generated card is used)
- Two-sided tape or tape squares
- Wire
- Wood handle with ½" hole
- Wood glue
- Matching colored card stock, two colors
- 20" length of ½" ribbon (in coordinating color)
- 12" lengths of wooden dowel: ⅜", ½"
- Craft paint (in coordinating color)

Tools

- Paper trimmer or rotary cutter and mat
- Decorative-edge scissors or corner punch
- Scissors
- Needle-nose pliers
- Wire cutter
- Hacksaw
- Paintbrush (optional)

Use that special Easter card you received last year as a garden greeting sign to place in a bucket of dried or fresh flowers. Cut, trim, and embellish the card with colored paper, wire, and ribbon. Add a dowel to insert the sign in a bucket of flowers.

COST: Under $10.00

TIME: 1 hour

- See photos for details and placement.

1 Cut pieces. Use a purchased Easter greeting card or create one with a computer and a card-making program. With paper trimmer, cut off the decoration on the front of the card and the verse on the inside of the card. Trim each piece to 3" x 4" or finished size you like. For first mat, cut two pieces of the first colored card stock ½" larger than decoration and greeting. For second mat, cut one piece of the second colored card stock ½" larger than the first colored card stock. Punch decorative corners if you like.

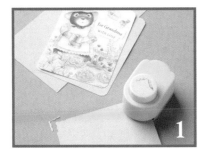

2 Adhere pieces. Tape the design in center of first mat. Center and glue first mat on top of second mat. In same way, double mat the verse. Tape the design and verse mats together back to back.

3 Cut and paint dowel. Cut a 12" length of ½" dowel using a hacksaw.

4 Make card holder. Cut a 12" length of wire. Gently fold it in half over the smaller ½" wooden dowel and hold both ends together with the pliers close to the dowel. Twist the dowel several times while holding the wire to make a small loop. Remove from the dowel. Separate the wire ends and separately wrap each end around the larger ⅜" dowel three to four times. Gently push the wire wraps closely together. Force the small circle end into the open end of the wooden handle. Position the wire wraps just above the wooden handle. Bend the two wire wraps so that they can hold the greeting sign. Place the sign in between the wire spheres.

5 Finish. Cut a 20" length of ribbon. Tie a bow over the top of the wooden handle close to the greeting sign. Cut ends at a slant. Insert the ½" dowel into the bottom of the wooden handle. Insert the dowel and greeting sign into a bucket of dried or fresh flowers.

Felt Egg Cozies

Materials

- 3" x 9" cream colored wool felt
- Embroidery floss: soft green, pastel to match ribbon
- 4" of ⅜" pastel satin ribbon
- Sewing thread to match ribbon
- Gold E-bead
- 7mm gold bee bead

Tools

- Air-erasable pen
- Needles: embroidery, hand sewing
- Scissors

Set a sweet table for Easter brunch with boiled eggs snuggled in embroidered felt egg cozies. Use a different color for each guest!

COST: $1.00 per cozy

TIME: 1 hour

- Enlarge pattern (see page 148) and cut out.
- See photos for details and placement.

1 Cut out patterns. Use pattern to cut out a front and back cozy piece from cream felt.

2 Embroider design. Transfer vine pattern onto cozy front with air-erasable pen. Use two strands of green floss to stem stitch over pattern lines and to make three single chain stitches at end of each stem.

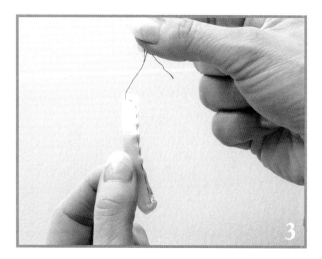

4 Add details. With same thread, pick up bead and sew it to flower center. Tack flower to vine as shown. Sew bee bead to background near flower.

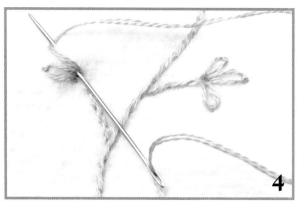

3 Make rosettes. Use single strand of thread to sew a running stitch in a wide U-shape along the ribbon. Pull thread to gather ribbon. Overlap ends with raw edges folded to back of flower. Knot thread and take a few tiny tack stitches to secure flower shape.

5 Stitch cozy. Use two strands of floss to blanket stitch bottom edge of cozy front. Without clipping floss, place front and back together, right sides out, and blanket stitch curved edges together. End by blanket stitching across bottom edge of cozy back.

Easter Tree

Materials

- 4" rose clay pot
- Acrylic craft paints: lavender, yellow, pink, green, blue
- Clear spray sealer (gloss or matte finish)
- Twigs (stripped of leaves)
- White spray paint
- Craft foam block to fit inside pot
- Small piece of cardboard
- Spanish moss
- Purchased Easter ornaments

Tools

- Flat ½" wide paintbrush
- Pencil with a flat eraser
- Hot-glue gun and glue sticks
- Scissors

Pastel paint and a few simple supplies are all that's needed to "sprout" a little Easter tree anywhere that your house could use some springtime cheer. Purchased or handmade ornaments complete the festive look.

COST: Under $20.00

TIME: 1 - 1½ hours

- Let paint and sealer dry thoroughly after each application.
- See photos for details and placement.

1 Paint clay pot. Paint pot with lavender paint, including 1" inside the top rim. Paint a second coat. Use paintbrush to paint alternating yellow, pink, green, and blue stripes on the top band of the pot, leaving a space in between each color the width of the brush to let the lavender show through. Paint stripes a second coat.

2 Paint details. Using the flat end of pencil eraser, paint yellow, pink, green, and blue polka dots in a random fashion on pot. Spray the pot with clear spray sealer.

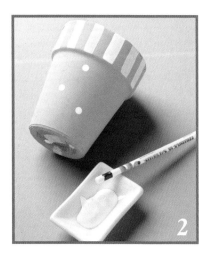

3 Prepare pot. Cut the craft foam block to fit inside the pot. Hot glue the foam block into the bottom of the pot. Cut a 4" cardboard circle to fit just inside the clay pot. Cut a hole in the middle of cardboard for the sticks. Hot glue the cardboard circle onto the top of the craft foam block.

4 Assemble. Spray the twigs using white spray paint. Paint pastel stripes on all of the twigs.

Spray with a clear spray sealer. Poke the sticks through the middle of the cardboard circle and into the foam. Hot glue moss around the sticks completely covering the cardboard circle. Decorate the tree with Easter ornaments.

cinco de mayo
Bright Appliquéd
Table Runner

Materials

- ½ yard bright Mexican print fabric
- ⅛ yard white fabric with Mexican designs
- White paper
- Optional: white fabric and adhesive appliqués
- Fusible fabric adhesive
- Black thread

Tools

- Compass
- Pencil
- Scissors
- Sewing machine

Celebrate Cinco de Mayo by setting the table with vivid colors and festive patterns. Torn fabric edges give the table runner a homespun look.

COST: $10.00

TIME: 30 minutes

- See photos for details and placement.
- See page 144 for stitches.

1 Cut circles. For pattern, use compass to draw a 4" diameter circle pattern on paper. Following the manufacturer's directions, fuse fabric adhesive to the back of the white fabric. When cool, trace around the circle pattern on the paper side of the fabric adhesive, centering circle over a design. Cut out six circles, three for each end of the table runner. Note: If using appliqués, apply them after the table runner is completed.

2 Make table runner. Tear an 18" x 36" piece from print fabric. Remove the paper backing from each circle and arrange three circles evenly spaced on each end of the table runner. Following the manufacturer's directions, iron the circles to the table runner.

3 Finish. Use black thread to zigzag stitch (see page 143) around each circle. Trim threads and iron the runner flat.

Cinco De Mayo

Cinco de Mayo, The 5th of May, commemorates the victory of the Mexican militia over the French army at The Battle of Puebla in 1862. It is primarily a regional holiday celebrated in the Mexican state capital city of Puebla. It is not, as many people think, Mexico's Independence Day, which is actually September 16.

51

Festive Beribboned
Treat Containers

Materials

- Small box with lid
- 12" x 12" print paper to match theme
- Invisible tape
- 8" of grosgrain ribbon: ⅞" red, bright pink, turquoise, ¼" lime green, 1¾" orange, ⅝" turquoise

Tools

- Hot-glue gun and glue sticks
- Scissors

Everyone will love finding treats nestled in these Cinco de Mayo favor boxes. Rows of grosgrain ribbon make brightly striped lids.

COST: $6.00 (unfilled box)

TIME: 45 minutes

- See photos for details and placement.

1 Cover box. Wrap bottom of box as you would a gift package. Use the box as a guide and cut the print paper just large enough so the paper covers the box completely. Trim paper even with the top edges of box. Use glue stick to glue the paper to the box.

3 Cover the lid. Cut enough ribbon pieces to cover the lid, allowing the ribbons to fold over the edges. Hot glue the ribbons to the lid, gluing only on the lid sides. Note: Work quickly to keep the glue from looking lumpy under the ribbon, pressing the ribbon to the glue immediately and firmly after applying glue. Cut a ribbon to fit around the side edges of lid. Glue in place.

2 Protect top edge. Tape the paper to the box around the top rim so that the paper doesn't tear as the box is opened and closed.

53

Mosaic Mat Board
Tiled Serving Tray

Materials

- 11" x 14" frame, at least 1" deep
- 11" x 14" white foam core board
- Spray paint: red, turquoise
- Drawer pulls with screws
- Mat board: red, yellow, aqua
- Matte spray finish
- Spray adhesive
- White texture

Tools

- Craft knife
- Sponge or soft cloth
- Scissors

Repurpose an old frame to make a festive party tray! A distressed frame will add to the rustic look.

COST: $25.00

TIME: 2 hours

- Let paint and finish dry thoroughly after each application.

1 Make tray. Remove glass and backing from frame. Spray front and back of frame with red paint. Spray drawer pulls with turquoise paint. Position pulls on opposite sides of tray and screw into place.

2 Cut mosaic pieces. Cut 11" x 14" piece of foam board. Spray red, yellow, and aqua mat board pieces with 3 coats of matte finish. With craft knife or scissors, cut yellow and red mat board in different shapes no larger than 1". For border, cut the aqua mat board into 1" squares.

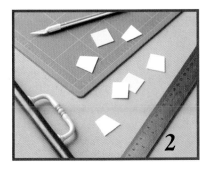

3 Adhere mosaic pieces. Spray top of white foam core board with a heavy coat of repositionable adhesive. For border, lightly position aqua tiles around the outside edge of the foam board. On inside of tray, spell out "fiesta" with red tiles. Fill in background with yellow tiles. Note: Use any word you like. Adjust and re-position as desired, leaving a little space between tiles. Press firmly in place to set.

4 Adhere mosaic pieces. Spread texture paste over tiled surface, making sure to work into cracks between tiles. Wipe excess paste off tiles with damp soft cloth or sponge soon after spreading, taking care not to lift tiles from design. Let dry overnight.

5 Finish. Insert glass in frame. Run a bead of clear drying glue around inside edge of tray and insert foam board. Note: If you like, protect bottom of tray with felt pads in the four corners.

Paper Confetti Eggs

Materials

- 2 dozen eggs
- Tissue paper (1 pkg. each): red, green, white
- Glue
- Water
- Plastic wrap

Tools

- Wooden skewer
- 1" sponge paintbrush
- Scissors

A Cinco de Mayo tradition is to gently smash confetti-filled eggs over fellow celebrants' heads. Join in the fun!

COST: $8.00

TIME: 1 hour

- See photos for details and placement.

1 Prepare eggs. Poke a hole in the top of an egg using the skewer. Widen the hole just enough to be able to break the yoke of the egg with the skewer. Empty the contents of the egg and rinse the empty shell under cold water. Turn upside down inside of the egg carton and set aside to dry.

2 Make the confetti. Layer three colors of tissue paper on top of each other and roll together tightly. Use the scissors to cut tissue paper into small confetti-sized pieces. Note: Set aside enough one-inch squares of white tissue paper to cover the holes in the top of eggs. Fill the hollowed out egg ⅓ full of confetti.

3 Cover egg hole. Mix glue and water in equal amounts. Place a square of white tissue paper over the hole at the top of the egg to seal in the confetti. Dip the paintbrush into the glue and paint glue over tissue.

4 Decorate egg with confetti. Paint the egg surface with glue and roll it in confetti. Set on a piece of plastic wrap to dry. Repeat process adding additional confetti if you like.

57

Materials

- 2" x 8" felt (for each): gold, gray (bottom piece)
- 2" x 8" felt (for each): cream, white (top piece)
- Embroidery floss: dark gray, cream
- Felt scraps: colors you like for berries
- Seed beads: color to coordinate with felt colors

Tools

- Sewing needle
- Beading needle
- Scissors

Felt scraps, beads, and delicate stitches combine to make beautiful bookmarks. No need to follow a pattern, make each one unique . . . just like Mom would.

COST: $5.00

TIME: 2 hours

- Use three strands of embroidery floss for all stitching.
- See photos for details and placement.

1 Cut felt pieces. Cut one 1¾" x 7¾" piece from gold and one from gray felt for bottom. Cut two 1 ⅜" x 7¼" pieces from cream felt for top.

2 Embroider branches. Cut an 18" length of dark gray embroidery floss. Use long straight stitches to make branches randomly on the top cream felt piece. See the photograph for stitching ideas.

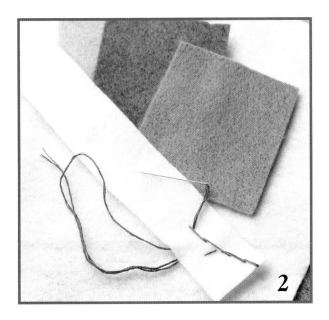

3 Make berries. Cut several pea-size circles from felt colors. With cream floss, make a French knot in the center of each felt piece to secure felt berries randomly along the stitched branches.

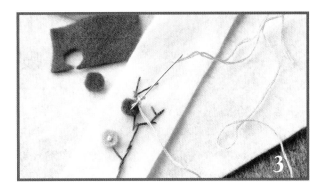

4 Attach beads. Use a beading needle and one ply of cream floss to sew seed beads randomly along the branches, grouping some together.

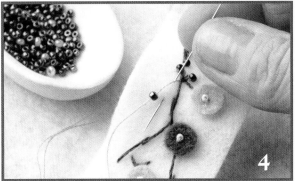

5 Assemble. Center the stitched top on the bottom. Use short, even running stitches to stitch the two felt pieces together along the straight edges of the top piece.

59

Gardening Apron

Materials

- *13" x 19" readymade place mat*
- *40" length of 1" ribbon (tie)*
- *20" of ⅜" coordinating ribbon*
- *Silk flower*
- *Fabric glue*

Tools

- *Safety pin*
- *Sewing machine*
- *Scissors*
- *Straight pins*

Stitch this quick-and-easy gardening apron from a place mat in Mom's favorite colors!

COST: $15.00

TIME: 1½ hours

- See figure (see page 149) for dimensions and stitching lines.
- See photos for details and placement.

1 Fold and mark apron. Fold place mat up 5" lengthwise and pin in place. Divide pocket of apron into sections as indicated in figure and mark with pins.

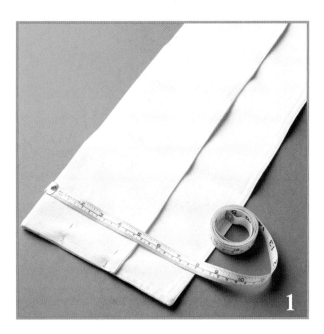

2 Attach ribbons. Pin or glue 1" ribbon along the top of the apron, ½" in from top outside edge of place mat. Fold a 4" loop of ribbon on one side to hold a gardening tool. Glue ⅜" ribbon along front of pocket, ¼" in from top edge of pocket.

3 Sew apron. Topstitch ¼" in along sides of apron, sewing across ribbons to secure them. Topstitch along pocket divider lines.

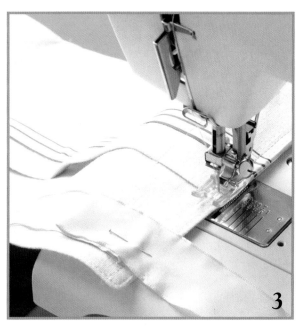

4 Finish. Pin silk flower accent to side of apron.

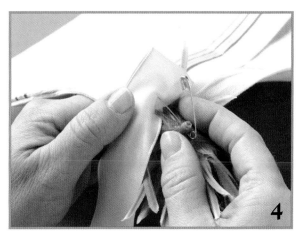

Bouquet of Flowers

Materials

- Tootsie Roll Pop suckers
- Green and red tissue paper, 1 sheet of each
- 4" x 7" green textured card stock
- 12" of ¾" green ribbon
- Green cloth-covered wire
- Green floral tape

Tools

- Black marker
- Pencil
- Wire cutter
- Scissors

Here's a truly "yummy" and thoughtful gift for Mom on Mother's Day! It is an easy and fun project for the whole family to make together. Make single flowers or a whole bouquet!

COST: $5.00 per bouquet

TIME: 30 minutes

- Trace and cut out pattern.
- See photos for details and placement.

1 Make leaf. Trace and cut leaf pattern from green card stock. Score leaf as indicated on pattern. Fold along line. Write message on leaf with a marker. For stem, cut a 5" length of green floral wire. To make a coil, wrap 2" of each wire around the stick of a sucker. Remove wire. Pierce a hole in the bottom of each leaf and insert the wire up to the spiral coil.

2 Wrap single flower. Wrap green floral tape in a spiral up and around stick of sucker. Lay wire of leaf along stick and wrap around it, too. Continue wrapping up to base of sucker. Tear off tape.

3 Wrap flower bunches. Tape three sticks together. Cut 5" squares of green tissue paper (one for each bunch). Fold the tissue into quarters without creasing edges. Poke a hole in the middle of tissue. Insert the sticks into the middle of paper and fluff tissue around suckers. (Photo 2) Wrap green floral tape in a spiral up and around sticks of suckers. Tear off tape.

4 Finish. Fold a half sheet of red tissue into a cone and wrap it around bundle of sucker flowers. Tie ribbon in a bow around sticks to hold tissue in place. Cut ends at a slant.

Dried Rose Votive

Materials

- Clay pots: 1 ¾", 3"
- 10" of 1" flat lace trim
- 3" block of floral foam
- 8 to 12 small dried roses
- Tea candle (Battery-operated tea candle is safer)

Tools

- Tape measure
- Glue gun and glue sticks
- Serrated knife
- Scissors

Give Mom this delicate-looking votive holder that is easy to make and looks very special. Add a hint of lace to a clay pot and use small dried roses of any color you like. Larger clay pots may also be used if you want a larger arrangement.

COST: $12.00

TIME: 45 minutes

- See photos for details and placement.

1 Attach lace. Cut a 10" length of lace edging. Place lace with straight edge along top edge of large pot. Use glue gun to place a dot of glue near top of pot and press end of lace over it. Let set. Continue gluing every inch or so in the same way. Overlap

place using glue gun.

3 Cut dried rose stems about 2" long at an angle. Remove extra leaves on stem and around blossom. Insert stems into space between pots, keeping them close together. Insert votive into small pot.

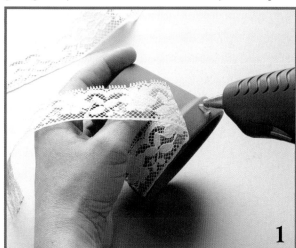

ends and cut lace.

2 Prepare pots. With serrated knife, cut floral foam into a 2½" square with a depth of 1". Cut off corners, angling slightly inward. Cut off more as needed until it fits snugly in the bottom of the large pot. Place small pot into center of large pot. Glue in

Memorial Day Pockets

Materials (one pocket)

- 8½" x 11" patriotic-print paper, 2 sheets
- Scrap of card stock
- 16" of ¼" package ribbon: red, blue
- 16" of ⅛" package ribbon: yellow
- Message stamp
- Black stamp
- Assorted wrapped candies
- Double-sided adhesive
- Glue

Tools

- ⅛" hole punch
- Pencil
- Ruler
- Scissors
- Scoring tool
- Decorative-edge scissors: mini scallop

A day of remembrance is a wonderful opportunity to show your support for local veterans. Create heart-shaped pockets filled with a friendly note of thanks as well as a treat or two. These pockets are great for May Day, too!

COST: $10.00

TIME: 1 hour

- Enlarge and cut out patterns (see page 149).
- See photos for details and placement.

1 Adhere two papers. Use double-sided adhesive to apply adhesive to back of one of the print papers. Press print papers together back to back.

2 Make pocket. Trace pocket pattern onto paper and cut out. Use a ruler and scoring tool to score lines on print paper as indicated on pattern. Fold along scored lines. Fold into heart shape pocket.

3 Make ribbon hanger. Punch a hole through all layers at inside center of heart. Thread ribbon through punched holes. Tie ribbons together in an overhand knot. Pull ribbon so knot is in center of pocket.

4 Make tag. Trace tag pattern on a scrap of two-sided print paper and cut out. Punch a hole as indicated on pattern. Stamp a message onto piece of card stock and cut out a rectangle using decorative-edge scissors. Glue message to front of tag. Slide tag onto ribbons. Fill pocket with wrapped candies, and it's ready to deliver.

Denim Fringed
Place Mat Napkin Set

Materials

- ½ yard light-weight denim, 60" wide
- 20" of red bandana cotton fabric
- Thread: navy, red

Tools

- Clear ruler
- Marking pencil
- Iron
- Scissors
- Sewing machine

These place mats are easy to make with minimal sewing. It's all in the fringing. True denim fringes easily and the fringe looks different in each direction. Add a fringed napkin in a coordinating print to complete the set.

COST: $7.00 for 2

TIME: 2 hours

- At beginning and end of stitching, pull thread to back and tie in a knot.
- Pre-wash all fabric. If fabric is not square, stretch it diagonally in the direction needed.

1 Make place mat. When fringing fabric, the fabric must be cut or torn on the straight grain.

To get the straight grain, clip into the selvage about 1" below the cut edge and tear across the fabric. Tear lengthwise along the selvage. Measure 14" down from the torn edge and mark fabric. Cut or tear. Measure 18" across this piece and cut fabric. Repeat one more time for two place mats. Note: The torn edge gives a more irregular look which is what you want for this project.

2 Make fringe. Pull out threads along all four sides of place mat until the fringe measures ½". Use a narrow zigzag stitch and navy thread to stitch along the edge of the fabric at the base of the fringe. Note: Use red thread if you want to show a contrast stitching.

3 Make flat-felled seam. Mark a line 3" in and 4" in from one short edge. Fold fabric, wrong sides together along the 3" line and press. Bring folded edge to the second line. Press and pin in place. Topstitch near the folded edge. Stitch another row of stitching ¼" from the first row, catching all 3 layers of fabric.

4 Make napkin. Use ruler to measure two 18" squares and tear or cut out. Fringe to ½" and stitch in same way as in Step 2.

Hanging Cones
with Floral

Materials

- 10" x 10" red/white/blue print fabric
- 9" x 9" fusible fleece
- 11" length of white ball fringe
- 12" of ⅜" navy grosgrain ribbon
- Small amount of each: fiberfill stuffing, wood excelsior
- White craft thread
- Permanent fabric adhesive

- Assorted silk flowers: red geraniums, blue carnations, white daisies
- 2 each of ¾" red and blue buttons
- 3¾" x 5¾" American flag on pole
- 12" (each) of 18-gauge plastic coated wire: red, white, blue

- Matching sewing thread
- ⅝" red wood bead with large hole
- 6" length of ⅜" wooden dowel (for curling wire)
- 2½" cardboard square (for wrapping tassel)

Tools

- Iron
- Straight pins
- Scissors
- Sewing machine or sewing needle

Stitch up a fabric cone and fill it with red, white, and blue flowers and a miniature flag for a cute wall pocket or decoration to hang on a doorknob'.

COST: $6.00

TIME: 90 minutes

- Enlarge and cut out pattern (see page 149).
- See photo for details and placement.

1 Trace and cut cone. Trace cone pattern onto fleece and cut out. Follow manufacturer's directions to fuse fleece to wrong side of print fabric. Cut out fabric along straight edges but leave ⅝" of extra fabric along curved edge.

2 Make cone. Pin straight edges together, right sides facing, and sew with ¼" seam allowance. Trim tip of cone. Turn right side out and fold top fabric edge to inside of cone. Glue in place.

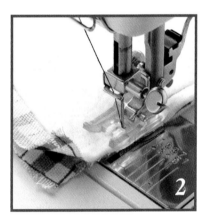

3 Add trims. Glue ball fringe to top outside edge, overlapping ends. For hanger, fold ribbon in half and glue ends to top inside of back of cone.

4 Fill cone. Stuff three-fourths of cone with fiberfill. Add a top layer of excelsior. Glue a button on center of each daisy or remove each daisy center and glue a button in its place.

Apply glue to flower stems and poke into excelsior. Wrap each wire around dowel to curl into spirals. Glue one end of each spiral inside arrangement. Poke flag pole into flowers at center.

5 Make tassel. Wrap craft thread around 2½" piece of cardboard 25 times. Carefully slip loops off cardboard and tie a 6" piece of thread through loops at one end of bundle. Clip thread loops on other end of bundle. Trim ends evenly. Apply glue sparingly to inside of bead. Insert tying thread through bead, pulling top of tassel into bead. Clip excess thread and glue bottom point of cone into top of bead.

Fish BBQ Apron

Materials

- Tan canvas butcher-block apron
- White paper (for stencil pattern)
- Disappearing tracing pen
- Fabric paints: copper, teal, gold, black

Tools

- Pencil
- Craft knife
- Straight pins
- Black marker
- Paper plate
- Natural sea sponge
- Small round paintbrush
- Scissors

Any beginning painter can create this painted fish on a purchased apron. Only two techniques are used—sponging and an easy brush stroke. Dad will enjoy having a personalized apron when grilling this summer.

COST: $10.00

TIME: 45 minutes

- Enlarge and cut out pattern (see page 150).
- Place paint on paper plate and dab sponge into it.
- Do not let paint dry between applications in order to blend colors.
- See photo for details and placement.

1 Make patterns. Trace pattern in center of white paper and cut out. Note: Cut pattern without stopping, so you have neat positive and negative patterns.

2 Paint eye. Cut out eye on positive pattern with craft knife, working on a protected surface. Center pattern on bib of apron and pin in place. Use black permanent marker to outline the eye. Remove pattern.

3 Sponge paint fish. Place negative fish pattern on apron aligning so eye is in the right place. Sponge center areas of fish with copper, avoiding the bottom and mouth area. Sponge the bottom of the fish gold. Sponge over all areas of the fish except the bottom area with teal.

4 Paint details. Paint the mouth area and any other small areas with the brush, dabbing paint on to get a similar look to the sponging. Some areas may be blended in this same way. Paint straight lines for top, side, and tail fins with black. Fill in the eye with black paint. Let paint dry 48 hours.

Dad's Place Bookmark

Materials

- ½" x 12" leather strips
- 30" length of 24-gauge copper wire
- Focal bead or charm
- Wood scrap
- Small beads including a ½" tubular shape
- 1 flat bead
- A few small round or shaped beads

Tools

- Ruler
- Awl
- Wire cutter
- Needle-nose pliers
- Scissors

Make this bookmark with a strip of leather, beads, and a special bead or a charm that depicts one of Dad's favorite pastimes or special interests. Charms are available in golf clubs, cowboy hats, footballs, and just about anything.

COST: $6.00

TIME: 1 hour

- See photos for details and placement.

1 Cut strips. Cut a ½" x 9" leather strip (for paperbacks) or ½" x 12" leather strip (for larger books). Cut one ½" x 2" strip.

Fold the 2" strip in half and use an awl to poke a hole in center of strip, protecting surface with a piece of wood. Cut a 9" piece of wire and insert it through the focal bead, leaving a 1" end beyond bead. Put a small bead on wire end and use needle-nose pliers to twist into a 2-loop coil, tucking the end to the inside. Thread the other end of wire through the hole in the 2" leather strip and twist a 2-loop coil close to the strip.

2 Attach bead and strip. Wrap the short strip around end of long strip. Holding the three layers together, wrap wire around all strips three times. With awl, poke a hole through all layers ½" from folded end and thread wire through from back to front. Insert wire into a flat bead and push it tightly against the leather. Poke a hole through all layers at end of bead and insert wire from front to back. Wrap wire around the leather strip two times. Insert wire between layers and cut excess.

3 Attach end beads. Cut one ½" x 1½" leather strip. At other end of long strip, fold 1½" strip in half. Cut an 8" length of wire. Insert wire halfway through tubular smaller bead on each wire end. Twist each wire into a 2-loop coil, tucking the ends to the inside. Cut excess wire.

4 Attach bead and strip. Use an 8" piece of wire and attach 1½" strip and a larger bead in same way as in Step 2.

Cigar Box Valet

Materials

- Wooden cigar box
- Tan mat board or card stock
- Green print paper to cover box
- White paper for label
- Metal corners (optional)

- Upholstery tacks
- Spray adhesive
- Foam core scrap
- Brown ink pad
- Library metal labels

- Two 18" lengths of ½" tan grosgrain ribbon
- Small piece of mini corrugated cardboard

Tools

- Stencil brush
- Hammer

What better gift for Dad than a box to hold all the "treasures" that he collects?

COST: $25.00

TIME: 2 hours

- See photos for details and placement.

1 Outside of box: Cover lid. Trim mat board or card stock to cover outside lid of cigar box. Note: Metal corners may be added to four corners of mat board. Round corners slightly with scissors and glue on metal corners. Adhere mat board to cigar box with spray adhesive. Cut slightly smaller piece of print paper. Rub brown ink on edges with stencil brush. Adhere paper to lid with spray adhesive.

2 Make label. With computer or by hand, print "Happy" (leave blank space for "Father's") and "Day". On separate paper, print "Father's" to fit in metal label. Trim and insert into label. Punch holes in paper on either side of first and last words as

shown in photo. Run ribbon through holes in paper and metal label. Cut piece of corrugated cardboard slightly larger than paper strip with message. Adhere tag to cardboard. Adhere cardboard to top of box.

3 Cover inside of box. Cut paper to fit in top and bottom of box. Ink edges with brown. Adhere papers to top and bottom of box with spray adhesive. Cut two pieces of ribbon to crisscross inside lid of box. Nail ribbon to box with upholstery tacks, one in each corner and one in the middle.

4 Make divider. Cut a piece from foam core to divide the box into two sections. Adhere paper on each side of foam core. Place dividers in box and add mementos, photos, stamps, reading glasses, pens, etc. Note: you can make more than one divider.

4th of july
Table Cover

Materials

- 2 red 1 ⅞" star buttons
- Seam sealant
- Pearl cotton, size 5: navy blue, white
- 28 white ½" buttons
- Permanent fabric adhesive
- 10 feet of ⅜" iron-on adhesive tape, ultra hold
- ½ yard blue/white stripe denim, 58" wide
- Trims, 1 yard each: red 1" chenille fringe, white 1¾" rickrack, red ⅞" grosgrain ribbon, navy ⅝" grosgrain ribbon, red ¾" rickrack

Tools

- Ruler
- Iron
- Scissors
- Fabric glue stick
- Embroidery needle

Make a festive table runner quick and easy with adhesives and bold embroidery stitches. A variety of trims add color and texture.

COST: $16.00

TIME: 2 hours

- Use glue stick to attach rickrack and ribbon trims to fabric before stitching.
- Begin and end stitches with knots on back side of runner.
- One strand of pearl cotton is used for all hand stitching.
- Glue ends of trim to runner with fabric adhesive after stitching is completed.
- See photos for details and placement.

1 Make runner. Cut a 17" x 58" piece from denim.

Follow manufacturer's directions to apply iron-on tape to both long edges of runner. Remove paper backing. Fold over along edge of tape and press hem in place.

2 Attach rickrack. Cut red fringe to fit across two short ends of runner. Apply seam sealant to cut ends. Let dry. Glue fringe to ends of runner. Position white rickrack ½" above fringe.

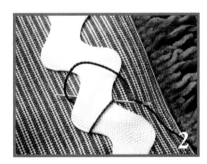

Insert navy pearl cotton into needle and knot one end of thread. Sew two diagonal straight stitches across every other point of rickrack to hold in place.

3 Attach ribbon and buttons. Cut navy and red ribbons to fit across two short ends of runner. Center navy ribbon on top of red ribbon and place ¾" above white rickrack. Insert white pearl cotton into needle and knot one end of thread. Sew buttons across ribbon ⅝" apart with one straight stitch between buttons. Sew eleven white buttons in place, then one red star button, then three more white buttons.

4 Attach rickrack. Cut red rickrack to fit across two short ends of runner. Place ¾" above ribbons. Insert white pearl cotton into needle and knot one end of thread. Sew one French knot on each tip of rickrack.

79

Wood Patriotic Flag

Materials

- Two 2" x 6" boards, 8 feet long
- Latex or craft acrylic paint: colonial blue, colonial red, white
- 1¼" star foam stamp
- 10 feet of 20-gauge copper wire
- Masking tape
- Marking pen
- Paper plate

Tools

- Table saw
- Circular or hand saw
- Drill and ⅛" bit
- Ruler
- Pliers with wire cutter
- 1" sponge brush
- Tape measure

This flag can be made from weathered boards or purchased lumber. The rustic patriotic symbol has 13 stars for the original 13 states.

COST: $11.00

TIME: 2 hours (not including drying time)

- Let paint dry thoroughly after each application.
- See photos and pattern (see page 150) for details and placement.

1 Cut boards. From each board, use a table saw to cut two boards 35" long, which will give you four boards. From each of these boards, use a table saw to cut 4 strips 1¼" wide. You will have 16 board strips measuring 1¼" x 1½". Cut each strip to measure 1¼" square. Cut one 20" length for the top hanging strip. Set it aside. From board scraps, cut 24 spacers ⅛" x 2".

2 Paint boards strips. Paint three sides of strips as follows: seven strips red and six strips white.

3 Assemble and drill boards. Lay the 13 board strips together, beginning with a red board and alternating colors. Place a spacer between strips at both ends. Make sure the top and bottom ends of boards are even. Mark drill holes at center of each strip, ½" from top. Drill holes. Center hanging strip along top edge. Lay a strip of masking tape lengthwise on the hanging strip for a guide to mark the center. Use the ruler to line up placement and mark a dot at edge of tape directly above each hole on strips. Drill holes in hanging strip. Drill two additional holes ½" in from outside edges of top hanging strip.

4 Attach wires. Cut 13 pieces of copper wire 7" long. Insert one wire through top of each strip front to back and through corresponding hole on hanging strip. Twist wires together at back but do not pull tightly. For hanger, cut a 30" piece of wire. Insert wire front to back in holes on each end of hanging strip. Wrap wire ends around hanging strip and twist wire around itself. Cut excess wire if necessary.

5 Paint star block. To determine the area to paint blue, measure down 14" from the top right corner and count in seven strips. Use masking tape to mark off this area. Paint the area blue. Mark placement for the 13 stars. Do not put stars on the outside blue stripes. Pour a puddle of paint on a plastic plate. Dip sponge in paint and blot twice before applying to wood. Stamp stars on wood.

Star Spangled Banner

Materials

- 10" x 20" stretched artist canvas
- 5" x 8" blue cotton fabric
- 4" x 5" red cotton fabric
- Red ⅝" button
- Matching thread
- Red embroidery floss
- Silk daisy

Tools

- Broad-tip permanent black marker
- Scissors
- Iron
- Sewing machine
- Glue gun and glue sticks
- Sewing needle

Write the words to your favorite patriotic song across an artist's canvas. Let simply sewn stripes and an artsy bloom dance center stage.

COST: $16.00

TIME: 45 minutes

- Use ¼" seam allowances.
- See photos for details and placement.

1 Write letters. With black marker, hold the artist canvas vertically and write the words to your favorite patriotic song in large cursive letters across the canvas. Allow the letters to flow off the page.

2 Cut and sew fabric. Cut two 3¼" x 5" pieces from blue fabric. Cut one 3½" x 5" piece from red fabric. Using ¼" seam allowances, sew a blue strip to the top and bottom of the red strip. Iron the seams flat.

3 Attach fabric. Lay the fabric piece on the center of the canvas. Lift each corner and place a small dot of hot glue on fabric and press down to hold in place.

4 Attach daisy. Remove center of daisy. Place daisy in the center of the red stripe. Insert red embroidery floss in needle and knot ends. Sew button to the center of the daisy. Knot and clip thread on back of daisy. Glue daisy on center of red fabric.

Patriotic Wreath

Materials

- Silver plastic plate charger
- Metallic gift bows (4 each): red, blue, silver
- 1" metallic red self-adhesive letters
- 4 feet of 2½" silver wire-edge ribbon
- Optional: Cardboard and a paper punch for hanger

Tools

- Glue gun and glue sticks
- Ruler
- Scissors

Your front door will glisten like fireworks with a metallic bow wreath. It can be your little secret that the main material in this glitzy greeting is dollar store bows.

COST: $16.00

TIME: 45 minutes

- See photos for details and placement.

1 Adhere letters. Peel "Happy Fourth of July" letters from their protective backings and position them slightly below the center of the plate charger. Note: To keep letters in a straight line, use a ruler as a guide.

2 Attach bows. To be sure the rim of charger will be entirely covered, arrange the bows around the wreath, grouping three like colors together. Leave a small space in the middle of the silver bows on the right of wreath for the ribbon bow. Remove backings from adhesive and press bows in place. Save two backings for the hanger. Note: If the backings will show on the charger or if you find the adhesive is weak, cut off the bow backings and use hot glue to adhere the bows to the charger.

3 Attach ribbon bow. Tie a large bow with silver ribbon. Cut ends at a slant. Hot-glue the ribbon bow in the space left between the silver gift bows.

4 Make hanger. Glue two of the bow backings together. Glue hanger to center back of charger. Note: You can also use a 1½" square of heavy cardboard with a hole punched near the top.

Materials

- Three 12" lengths of ³⁄₁₆" dowels
- Pre-made painted wood floral frames
- Light sage acrylic paint
- Wallet photos
- Silk flowers in colors of your choice
- 1 yard of ¾" sheer green ribbon
- Vase

Tools

- Paintbrush
- Saw
- Glue gun and glue sticks
- Scissors
- Photocopier (optional)

Plant your kids' pictures among pretty blooms this Grandparents Day. Pre-made frames make it easy to do—you just add the stem!

COST: $6.00 for three stems; $30 with vase of flowers.

TIME: 1 hour for 3 picks

- Let paint dry thoroughly after each application.
- Remove labels from the pre-made floral frames.
- See photos for details and placement.

1 Paint dowels. Use paintbrush to paint the dowels light sage. Paint a second coat if needed.

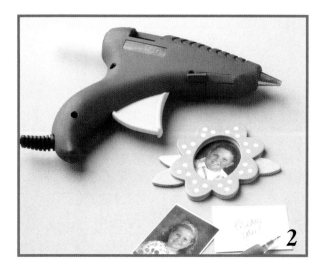

2 Insert photos. Cut the photos to fit in frame openings, allowing a border for gluing. Note: If needed, enlarge or reduce the size of the photos to fit the frame on a photocopier. Write a message to fit into one frame opening if you like. Glue photos and message to show through each frame opening.

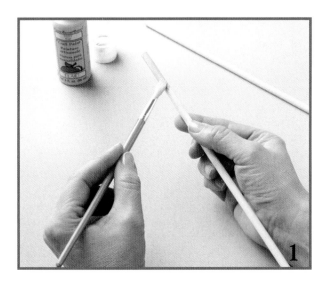

3 Attach dowels. Hot-glue one end of one dowel securely to the back of each frame.

4 Finish. Arrange silk flowers in the vase. Poke the photo picks into the arrangement. Tie ribbon in a bow around the neck of the vase. Cut ribbon ends at a slant.

Laced Treat Tray

Materials

- *Square plastic plate or tray with pattern you like*
- *2 yards of ½" ribbon to coordinate with plate*

Tools

- *Ruler*
- *Marking pen*
- *Electric drill*
- *Large drill bit*
- *Safety goggles*
- *Glue gun and glue sticks*
- *Scissors*

Bringing Grandma and Grandpa sweet treats will seem even more special when served on a special platter they can use again and again.

COST: $5.00

TIME: ½ hour

- See photos for details and placement.

1 Measure holes. Determine where you want the lacing on the plate. Note: The lacing can go all around the plate, run down one side, or be in one corner as shown. Lay a ruler over the front of the plate and with a marking pen, make marks 1" apart.

3 Insert ribbon. Trim the ribbon on one end to a point to make lacing easier. Insert the point into an end hole on the plate from front to back and begin lacing in and out. Be sure pattern of ribbon is right side up. If you want a bow on the corner of the plate as shown, cut a ribbon piece for each side and have them join in the corner. Tie ribbon in a bow. Trim ends at a slant.

4 Finish. On the back of the plate, trim the ribbon tails to 1". Adhere them to the plate using a glue gun.

2 Drill holes. Put on safety goggles. Use a drill to carefully drill holes where marked. Place a board beneath tray to protect working surface.

Family Tree

Materials

- 4" terra-cotta pot
- Bush or tree branch
- Masking tape
- White acrylic paint
- Blue spray paint
- 4" square floral foam
- Blue flat glass marbles
- Card stock: ivory, copper
- Optional: Purchased tags
- Heart-shaped copper paper clips
- 16" of ¼" gold trim
- Glue dots
- Photos

Tools

- 1" sponge paintbrush
- Decorative-edge scissors: mini scallop
- Glue gun and glue sticks
- Serrated knife
- Scissors

Hang favorite family photos from your very own family tree, chosen from your backyard. Simple black and white photo tags hang from copper paper clips.

COST: $15.00

TIME: 1½ hours

- Let paint dry after each application.
- See photos for details and placement.

1 Prepare branches. Choose a branch that will accommodate hanging many pictures. Note: You may want to use several branches together. Bind the branches together by wrapping masking tape around them. Spray-paint the branches blue.

2 Prepare pot. Paint the terra-cotta pot using the sponge brush and white paint. Paint the outside as well as inside the top edge of pot. Paint the pot with a second coat of white paint. Use a serrated knife to trim floral foam to fit snugly into the pot. Add a drop of glue to bottom of foam before pressing it into the pot.

3 Add ribbon trim. Thread ribbon through the center of six heart-shaped paper clips. Wrap ribbon around the top band of pot and tie ends together. Trim ends of ribbon.

4 Insert branches. Press branch or branches into floral foam. Remove them, apply glue to ends, and insert back into same holes. Glue flat glass marbles on top of floral foam.

5 Make tags. Cut out tags on copper-colored card stock. Choose photos and cut them to fit on tags. Glue photos to ivory card stock. Trim edges of card stock with decorative-edge scissors, leaving a ⅛" border. Glue photos to center of tags.

6 Hang tags. Attach a paper clip to the top of each tag and hang from the branches.

halloween
Felt Trick-or-Treat Bag

Materials

- Felt pieces:
  2 orange 9" x 12"
  3 green ¾" x 8"
  1 black 4" x 7"
- 2 pink 1⅛" buttons
- 2 white 2¼" buttons
- 24" of purple ⅛" grosgrain ribbon
- 1 yard ⅝" grosgrain ribbon:
  white, black

Tools

- Black fine-point marker
- Tracing paper
- Pencil
- Ruler
- Scissors

Making this goody bag just couldn't be easier! Just cut and glue to make your child a one-of-a-kind bag to gather of all of those yummy treats on Halloween night.

COST: $5.00

TIME: 40 minutes

- Enlarge and cut out patterns (see page 151).
- See photos for details and placement.

1 Cut felt. For bag, cut two 9" x 12" pieces from orange felt. To round bottom corners of felt, measure 2" in from each corner and make a mark.

1A

Draw a curve between marks. Cut curves. Trace face patterns on black felt and cut out. Trace hair pattern on green felt and cut out. For fringe, cut narrow slits along curved edge as indicated on pattern.

1B

2 Decorate bag. Use marker to draw two long lines down length of pumpkin, curving line in slightly at bottom. Arrange face pieces on pumpkin and glue in place. Glue pink buttons on for cheeks. Glue white buttons on for eye accents. Glue hair on top of pumpkin.

3 Make bow. Tie purple ribbon in a multi-loop bow with six 1½" loops and 3" tails. Glue bow in center of hair.

4 Assemble pumpkin. Glue front and back pumpkin pieces together along outer edges of sides and bottom, leaving top open. Trim edges if needed.

5 Make handles. Cut two 18" lengths of ⅝" ribbon. Glue ends of one ribbon on inside top of pumpkin back, 1?" in from outside edges. Glue other ribbon to inside of pumpkin front in same way. Note: To reinforce handles, take several stitches through ribbon ends and felt with needle and thread.

5

Studded Pumpkin

Materials

- Pumpkin
- Black and white flower brads: 1 large, five small
- Long straight pin
- 30" of 1¼" black/white polka-dot ribbon
- Silver upholstery tacks

Tools

- Pencil
- Scissors

Use upholstery tacks for instant pumpkin pizzazz. You can create a swirl, initials, faces, or whatever "spooktacular" designs you conjure up!

COST: $13.00

TIME: 20 minutes

- See photos for details and placement.

1 Make design dots. Use a sharpened pencil to gently poke holes approximately 1" apart to outline the spiral design.

2 Insert tacks and brads. Using the pencil marks as guides, push the upholstery tacks and flower brads into the pumpkin. Note: For brads, keep both prongs straight and together. Gently push into the pumpkin. If the prongs tend to bend, pre-poke a hole with an upholstery tack.

3 Attach bow. Tie ribbon in a bow. Cut ends at a slant. Insert a long straight pin through the back of the knot. Insert pin into top center of pumpkin.

Draped Candelabra

Materials

- Old candelabra-type votive candleholder
- Black spray paint
- 2 square yards of cheesecloth
- Black acrylic craft paint
- Small bat stamp
- Freezer or wax paper
- 12" x 18" black foam sheet
- Light marking pencil
- Three 18" lengths of 20-gauge stem wire
- 5 votive candles
- Paper plate

Tools

- Glue gun and sticks
- Scissors

Use an old candelabra to create a great Halloween centerpiece. There are many variations on this theme. Some of the elements could be used to decorate a hanging ceiling light fixture.

COST: $11.00

TIME: 45 minutes (not including drying time)

- Enlarge and cut out pattern (see page 151).
- Let paint dry after each application.

1 Paint candelabra. Spray-paint an old candelabra black.

2 Stamp bats. Place length of cheesecloth on a paper-covered surface. Pour a small puddle of black paint on a paper plate. Dip bat stamp in paint and dab it on plate before stamping on cheesecloth. Stamp bat shapes randomly on cheesecloth.

3 Make large bats. Enlarge bat pattern to measure 7" across. Use light marking pencil to trace three bats on black foam and cut out.

Cut stem wire into 10", 12", and 14" lengths. Use glue gun to glue top end of each wire to back of a bat shape. Note: Bat shapes can be two-sided by cutting out three more bats and gluing the wire between two pieces.

4 Finish. Use glue gun to glue ends of bat wires to a votive or wrap wire around the candelabra. Drape cheesecloth around base of candelabra.

Boo'tiful Crocheted Treat Bag

Materials

- 3 yards white lightweight fabric
- Felt scraps: white, black
- ⅔ yard ⅛" orange ribbon
- ⅔ yard ¾" green dot
- Fabric glue

Tools

- Size Q crochet hook
- Yarn needle
- Pencil
- Scissors

Simple crochet stitches transform fabric strips into a fun Halloween treat bag. Add friendly facial features for fun trick or treating.

COST: $10.00

TIME: 2 hours

- Trace and cut out patterns (see page 152).
- See photos for details and placement.
- Recycled bed sheets work well for this project.

1 Prepare strips. Tear fabric into 1" wide strips the length of the fabric. Join strips together in an overhand knot. Wind strips into a ball in same way as yarn.

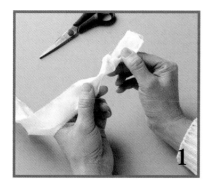

2 Crochet bag. With crochet hook, chain 18 stitches. Single crochet into each chain stitch. Continue with single crochet until the piece measures approximately 22" long.

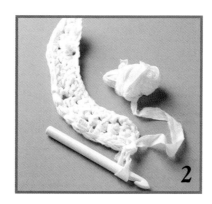

3 Sew side seams. Trim the fabric strip end to 18" and insert through a yarn needle. Fold crocheted piece in half with wrong sides together. Weave the needle back and forth through the stitches along the side seam. At the bottom edge, tie a knot and add a drop of glue. Trim ends of fabric strip close to knot. Use an 18" length of fabric strip to weave the other side seam together in the same way.

4 Make handle. Tie the end of fabric strip to the top left edge of bag. Use crochet hook to chain 24 stitches. Make a slip stitch to attach chain to the opposite edge of bag. Single crochet in each chain stitch. Repeat for a total of three rows. Finish by knotting the fabric strip through a crochet stitch. Add a drop of glue.

5 Hide knot ends. For a more finished look, use the crochet hook to weave ends of fabric knots between the crocheted stitches. Add a drop of glue and trim fabric ends.

6 Make face. Trace patterns for facial features onto black and white felt as indicated on patterns and cut out. Use fabric glue to adhere features to front of bag.

7 Finish. Place narrow ribbon on center of wide ribbon. Tie ribbons in a bow. Cut ends at a slant. Glue bow to top of bag. Note: You can also tie bow around base of one handle.

Creepy Crawly Soap Bars

Materials

- Glycerin soap
- Plastic microwavable cup
- Plastic bugs
- Soap molds or empty plastic containers
- Soap dye: red, yellow

Tools

- Microwave
- Stir stick

Clean up those sticky Halloween candy hands with fun plastic bugs embedded in glycerin soap.

COST: $10.00

TIME: 1 hour

- See photos for details and placement.

1 Prepare soap. Cut glycerin soap into 1" squares.

Place into a microwavable cup and melt, following the manufacturer's directions. Add one drop of coloring at a time and stir.

For orange color, add one drop at a time of red and yellow coloring until the orange color is as you like it.

2 Make soap. Place plastic bug into the bottom of mold. Fill mold with melted soap covering the bug. Set aside to cool. Note: to speed cooling, the soap may be refrigerated.

3 Make candy-corn soap. To make soap with three layers of colors (orange, yellow, and clear), set plastic bug into mold. Fill ⅓ full with orange soap. Let cool. Fill mold another ⅓ full with yellow soap. Let cool. Fill the mold to the top with clear soap. Let cool.

"Reely" Creepy Invitation

GHOSTS!

IT'S GOING TO BE "REELY" creepy

BOO!

COME TO
OUR HAUNTED BARN FOR
A HALLOWEEN FILM FESTIVAL
ALL HALLOWS EVE 2006
WITCHING HOUR: 8 PM

BE READY FOR SPOOKY SURPRISES!
BRING YOUR FLASHLIGHT

Materials

- Old film reel and case
- 5" x 8" vellum
- 5" square paper: 2 Halloween theme, 1 black
- Ghost foam stamp
- White stamp pad
- Thick craft glue
- 12" of ¼" orange gingham ribbon
- Round metal-rimmed key tag
- Round "Boo" word sticker
- Metal button with Halloween word
- Metal Halloween charm
- Dimensional foam dots
- Spray adhesive

Tools

- Decorative-edge scissors: grass
- ⅛" hole punch
- Compass
- Orange marker

Decorate an old film reel and case to invite your family and friends over on Halloween for some scary movies and games!

COST: $15.00

TIME: 1 hour

- See photos for details and placement.

1 Decorate tin. Use compass to draw a 5" circle on black paper. Cut out. Randomly stamp a ghost image with white ink on the black circle. Print out the invitation information on vellum, using a spooky font. Note: Font used in sample is "Creepy." Draw a 4½" circle around words. Cut out circle with the decorative scissor. Adhere vellum to black circle with spray adhesive. Glue invitation to front of film case.

2 Add trims. Affix sticker to center of metal rimmed key tag. Punch ⅛" hole in top of tag. Insert orange gingham ribbon through metal cat charm and hole in key tag. Tie ribbon in a knot. Cut ends at a slant. Place foam dot on back of key tag and press to front of reel tin.

3 Decorate reel. Use compass to draw a 5" circle on pattern paper. Cut out. Adhere to bottom of reel so you see it from the top. For tag, cut 2" x 3" piece of white card stock. Print on vellum, "It's going to be reely." Trim vellum to 2" x 3" and adhere to tag with spray adhesive. Tear 2" x 3" scrap of pattern paper. Tear in half diagonally. Highlight one edge with orange marker. Glue to bottom of white tag. Adhere a metal charm to tag with a foam dot. Punch a hole in upper left corner of tag. Insert a ribbon into hole and tie in a knot. Cut ends at a slant. Glue tag to front of reel.

103

Spooky Wreath

Materials

- 20" artificial evergreen wreath
- 8 wooden 3" to 5" Halloween shapes
- Spray paint: black, white
- "Glow-in-the-dark" paint
- 50" of monofilament line
- ⅜ yard Halloween print fabric (bow)
- 44" of ⅛" black ribbon (hangers)
- 1 bag of spider web
- Wire for hanging wreath

Tools

- Small paintbrush
- Paper plate
- Wire cutter
- Scissors
- Drill and bit if needed
- Sewing machine

Use an old evergreen wreath and recycle it into a fun and spooky Halloween wreath. Use "Glow-in-the-dark" paint to make it even spookier in the dark.

COST: $15.00

TIME: 45 minutes

- See photos for details and placement.
- Let paint dry thoroughly after each application.

1 Prepare wreath. Spray wreath with black paint using most of the can. Move tips around, uncovering unpainted areas and spray again. Note: Cover a large area with old newspaper and spray in a well ventilated area.

2 Paint wood shapes. If any pieces do not have a hole for hanging, drill one. Spray wooden shapes with white paint. Paint a top coat with "glow-in-the-dark" paint. Cut ⅛" ribbon into 4" lengths, one for each wood shape. Insert one end of each ribbon though hole in top of each wooden shape. Pull ends evenly and tie together in an overhand knot.

3 Make bow. Cut two 6" x 44" fabric strips from selvage to selvage. Sew short ends together with right sides together to create one long piece. Cut 1" irregular slits in the ends of the fabric. Cut angled slashes along the sides and even some holes in the center of fabric. Tie fabric in a bow. Glue on top of the wreath.

4 Finish. Drape spider web lightly around wreath.

Skeleton Topiary

Materials

- Acrylic paint: orange, lime green, purple, black, white
- 3" terra-cotta flowerpot
- 2 ½" craft foam ball
- 12" length of ¼" wide black and white striped cord
- Solid foam artificial pear
- 24" lengths of ⅝" wide Halloween ribbon
- Shredded paper in Halloween colors
- 7½" length of ⁵⁄₁₆" dowel

Tools

- Flat paintbrush
- Table knife
- Pencil
- Hot-glue gun and glue sticks

These silly fellows look full of tricks and treats. The skeleton heads are made from inverted pears propped up on trim-wrapped dowels.

COST: $8.50

TIME: 1¼ hours

- See photos for details and placement.
- Trace and cut out patterns (see page 151).
- Let paint dry after each application.

1 Paint flowerpot. Use color of your choice to paint below the rim. Use a flat paintbrush to make a dotted rim with black paint.

2 Cut foam. Trim off a slice from each foam ball approximately ¼" deep. With the flat side up, hot-glue the ball into the flowerpot.

3 Decorate dowel. Paint the dowel black. Wrap the dowel with cord, tacking in place with hot glue.

4 Insert dowel. Pull off the stem and leaves from the pear. Poke the sharp point of a pencil into the hole where the stem was. Hot-glue one end of a dowel into the small end of the pear.

5 Paint pear. Paint the entire pear white. Paint a second coat if needed. Use black paint to paint a simple, silly face on the skeleton. Note: You may want to draw face lightly in pencil first and then paint over pencil lines.

6 Finish. Tie ribbon in a bow around dowel just under the pear. Cut ends at a slant. Tack in place with hot glue. Fill the flowerpot with shredded paper to cover the foam.

Fabric Pumpkin

Materials

- ⅓ yard of orange print fabric
- Scrap of tan print fabric
- Newspaper
- One roll of toilet tissue paper
- Scraps of quilt batting
- 3 artificial leaves
- 15" of gold wire

Tools

- Wire cutter
- Sewing machine or needle and thread
- Wooden dowel
- Glue gun and glue sticks
- Scissors

Have fun making several adorable pumpkins to create a whole pumpkin patch for Halloween with just fabric, tissue, batting, and newspaper.

COST: $10.00

TIME: Under 1 hour

- See photos for details and placement.

1 Make circle pattern. Fold a large sheet of newspaper diagonally four times to create a pie-shaped piece. Measure 8" from the tip on each side of the pie shape and mark with a pencil. Cut the paper by cutting a very slight arc from one mark to the other. Open the paper and trim slightly if edges are not even. Pin the circle pattern to the orange fabric and cut out.

2 Prepare fabric cover. Baste around the outside edge of the circle using a sewing machine or needle and thread. Slightly gather the basted stitches to create a bowl-like shape.

3 Shape pumpkin. Cut quilt batting into 2" x 12" strips. Tuck one end of the strip into hole at the top of a roll of tissue paper. Wrap strip around the roll, tucking the other end of the strip into the hole at the top of the roll on the other side. Repeat this step until the roll of tissue paper has the shape of a pumpkin. Note: Use more batting for larger pumpkins. Place the wrapped roll in the center of the gathered fabric. Using fingers, slight pleat the fabric and tuck it into the hole on the top of the roll all the way around the fabric. Adjust the pleats so they are evenly spaced.

4 Make stem. Cut a 4" x 6" rectangle from tan fabric. Fold the fabric with right sides together to measure 2" x 6". Sew together along one 2" end and the 6" side. Trim corners, turn, and press. Cut a strip of newspaper about 6" wide and 20" long. Starting with the 6" end of the paper, roll it into a rod. Put the rod into the fabric stem. Use more or less newspaper to fill the stem completely. Fold the unfinished end over and glue the rod into the hole on top of the pumpkin.

5 Finish. Glue three silk leaves into the hole next to the stem. Wrap a 15" length of wire around wooden dowel to create a curled wire, leaving a straight 1" end. Glue the wire end in the hole next to the stem.

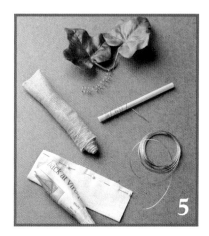

Felt Wallhanging

Materials

- Felt:
  - 16" x 20" black
  - 5" x 6" gray
  - 2" x 3" green
  - 4½" x 5" orange
  - 3½" x 9" tan
  - 8" x 12" white
  - 3" x 3" yellow
- Adhesive pre-cut felt letters
- Black buttons (2 each):
  - ⅜", ¼"
- 2 black ⅜" buttons
- 2 black ¼" buttons
- 6" of purple ⅛" grosgrain ribbon
- 5 purple ½" buttons
- 3 black/white 1" flower buttons
- 1 black ¾" spider button
- 1 candy corn button
- Tree limb, approximately 20"
- Glue
- 1¼ yard grosgrain ribbon (of each):
  - ⅛" purple
  - ⅜" orange
  - ⅜" green
- Disposable plate or bowl
- Orange bead/disc trim
- Black acrylic craft paint
- Tracing paper

Tools

- #10/0 liner brush
- Pencil
- Straight pins
- Scissors
- Ruler or yardstick
- Black fine-line permanent marker

Create this comical ghost to scare off the goblins lurking around the corners of your haunted abode.

COST: $7.00

TIME: 1 hour

- Enlarge and cut out patterns (see page 152).
- See photos for details and placement.
- Let paint dry thoroughly after each application.

1 Paint faces. On bead/disc trim, paint triangles for eyes and nose on each disc with black. Paint curved line for mouths. Repeat on reverse side.

2 Cut felt pieces. Pin patterns to appropriate felt colors and cut out.

3 Make hanging. Cut a 16" x 18" piece of black felt for hanging background. For casing, make a paper pattern for cutting tabs in the top of hanging. Draw five 2" x 4" tabs with 1½" spaces between them. Draw a point on the end of each tab. Pin the pattern on top of hanging and cut out tabs.

4 Attach pieces. Arrange pieces on hanging and glue in place. Glue word of choice ("Boo," "Welcome," etc.) on hanging. Glue on buttons, removing shanks if needed. Use black marker to add details to tombstones, pumpkin, and ghost as indicated on pattern. Make a bow with purple grosgrain ribbon and glue on ghost. Cut ends at a slant.

5 Finish tabs. Fold tabs in half and pin to the top edge of the hanging. Glue in place. Glue a purple button to each tab. Note: Buttons can also be hand sewn in place.

6 Finish. Glue beaded/disc trim to bottom edge of hanging. Insert stick through tab loops. For hanger, hold three ribbons together and tie in knot around each end of stick.

thanksgiving
Candle Floral Arrangement

Materials

- Goblet-type wine glass
- One 3" floral foam block
- Artificial fall leaves (1 bunch each): orange, red, brown
- 1 bunch of large orange flowers
- 1 bunch of medium burgundy flowers
- 1 bunch of small light orange flowers
- 1 bunch yellow berries
- 12" taper candle
- 4 feet of 1¼" wired orange plaid ribbon
- Masking tape

Tools

- Ruler
- Serrated knife
- Glue gun and glue sticks
- Chopstick or pencil
- Wire cutter
- Scissors

Turn a wine glass into a small Thanksgiving arrangement that includes a fragrant candle with a variety of fall-colored artificial flowers and berries in shades of burgundy, orange and yellow to celebrate the season.

COST: $25.00

TIME: 1 hour

- See photos for details and placement.

1 Prepare foam. Measure top and depth of glass and cut foam to fit. Cut off bottom edges of foam, rounding it to fit bottom of glass. Foam should be about ½" above top of wine glass.

Mark center of foam for candle placement. Use pencil to trace around base of candle onto foam. Use tip of serrated knife to cut a 1" deep hole for candle. Wipe glass clean of any floral foam residue.

2 Line glass. Cut leaves from stems. Apply glue to base of leaf with glue gun. Press base of leaf to bottom of glass. Use a chopstick (or pencil) to hold base of leaf in place until secure. Repeat until leaves cover the inside of the glass. Remove any glue tendrils with a blow drier. Insert candle in foam. Insert foam into the glass. Note: Tape overhanging leaves to the outside of the glass to keep them out of the way when inserting the foam.

3 Arrange florals. Tie ribbon in a bow around the base of the candle. Cut ends at a slant. Cut stems of three larger flowers 5" long. Bend the stems curving into a partial circle. Insert one into the foam in front of the bow. Insert others toward the back and side. Cut the medium-sized flower stems 3" long and insert near and around the candle. Cut the multi small flower stems 2" to 6" long. Insert on both sides, having them angle downward. Cut berry stems 4" to 5" long. Insert randomly. Reshape bow.

Happy Thanksgiving Wreath with Feathers

Materials

- 24" wispy twig wreath
- 16" length of holiday glittered fruit pick in neutral colors
- 4 peacock-eye feathers: 9" to 12" long
- 4½" x 5" pheasant feather pad
- 4" length of medium-weight wire

Tools

- Wire cutter
- Glue gun and glue sticks

Let autumn colors sparkle on a wreath you can enjoy the entire season. Peacock feathers dot the wreath with a hint of unexpected color and flair.

COST: $25.00

TIME: 1 hour

- See photos for details and placement.

1 Glue on fruit. When choosing a twig wreath, look for one that is fairly symmetrical. Decide on the position of the glittered fruit pick on the twig wreath, keeping a uniform roundness in mind. On a protected work surface, hot-glue the fruit pick to the wreath. Be careful of glue dripping through the twigs.

2 Glue on peacock feathers. Arrange three peacock feathers branching out from the top of the fruit and one branching out from the bottom. Lift the leaves of the fruit pick and glue the base of each feather in place. Let cool. Add more glue if needed.

3 Glue on feather pad. Tuck the pheasant feather pad next to the fruit pick, pointing feathers toward the center of the wreath. Hot-glue the pad in place.

4 Make hanger. Insert 4" length of wire into back of wreath. Make a loop with wire and twist ends together.

Painted Wood Candlesticks

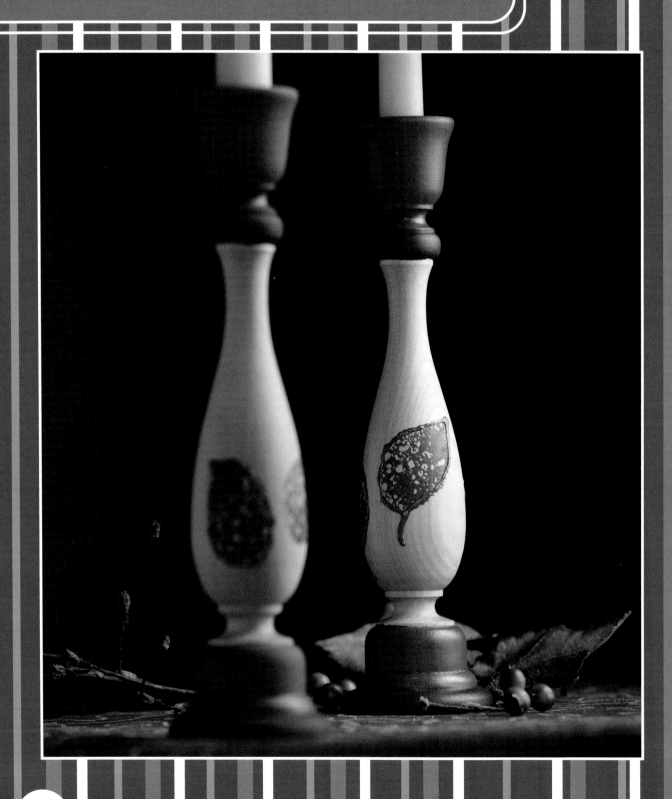

Materials

- 9" wooden candlesticks
- White spray primer
- Craft acrylic paints: burgundy, burnt orange, brown
- 3-D burnt orange paint
- Clear-finish spray
- Paper plate
- Paper towel cardboard center
- Masking tape
- Plastic wrap
- Paper
- Compressed sponge

Tools

- Pencil
- ¼" paintbrush
- Scissors

Create "one-of-a-kind" painted candlesticks, combining painted sections, sponged leaves, and 3-D paint. Choose Thanksgiving colors such as burgundy, burnt orange, and brown and insert coordinating candlesticks.

COST: $10.00

TIME: 1½ hours

- Trace and cut out pattern (see page 153).
- Let paint dry thoroughly after each application.

1 Paint tops and bottoms. Spray entire surface of candlesticks with primer. Cover and tape center area of candlestick, leaving top and bottom exposed. Use acrylic paint to paint each ring of the top and bottom of candlestick a different color. Paint additional coats as needed. Note: For bottom areas, it is easier to hold the brush stable and turn the candlestick.

2 Prepare sponge. Trace leaf pattern on compressed sponge and cut out. Drop sponge into water to expand. Squeeze out excess water and let dry slightly.

3 Sponge leaves. Uncover center area of candlestick. Using paper leaf pattern to determine placement of leaves. Note: Practice sponging on a paper towel cardboard center to get the sponging movement on a rounded surface. To sponge, put a drop of paint on the paper plate. Place sponge in paint and dab it off to the side to equally distribute paint. Sponge the leaf designs on candlestick using a quick rolling motion.

4 Outline leaves. Using the 3-D paint, outline the sponged leaves one at a time. Let each dry in a horizontal position before doing the next one. Note: Place your hand on a thick book and anchor your hand on the bottom of the candlestick to achieve stability when working. Since leaves are natural, they do not need to be sponged or painted perfectly.

Embellished Basket

Materials

- 8½" x 6" x 6¾" Chipwood basket with handle
- Wool felt: 9" x 12" sheet of four assorted fall colors
- 3 yards of plaid 1½" wide wire-edged ribbon
- Dark brown embroidery floss
- Double-stick tape
- 12 glass beads: 7 to 12mm in assorted fall colors
- 17" of 20-gauge wire
- 8" of thin wire (26-30 gauge)
- 48" of brass colored plastic-coated 22-gauge wire
- Permanent fabric adhesive

Tools

- Wire cutter
- Embroidery needle
- Ruler
- Toothpick
- Pencil
- Scissors

Beautiful fall colors are repeated in felt, ribbon, wire, and glass beads to make this basket accent for the Thanksgiving table.

COST: $8.00

TIME: 2 hours

- Enlarge and cut out pattern (see page 153).
- See photos for details and placement.

1 Make leaves. Use leaf pattern to trace and cut out six pairs of leaves from assorted colors of felt. Cut 20-gauge wire into six 4¼" pieces. Cut 4¼" piece of double-stick tape and press sticky side to center of one felt leaf, starting ¼" from bottom edge. Remove liner from tape and press one wire down center of adhesive.

Press matching leaf over leaf with wire, matching edges. Repeat with remaining leaf pairs and wires. Use two strands of dark brown floss to blanket stitch around edges of each leaf.

2 Make bow. Make a multi-loop bow with ten 2½" loops and 12" tails. Wrap ribbon center with 8" length of thin wire to secure. Cut ends at a slant. Wrap wire around handle to attach bow to basket.

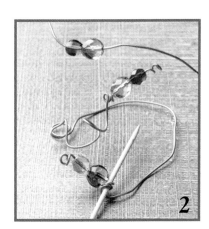

3 Make bead accents. Cut brass wire into three 16" lengths. Wrap one end of wire around a toothpick to make several tight coils. Insert wire into two

different-colored beads. Make two coils in wire using toothpick in same way as before. Repeat for all three wires. Wrap two wires around loops of bow and one around handle below bow.

4 Finish. Arrange ribbon tails on basket front in wavy pattern. Glue in place. Arrange leaves around bow and glue in place. Note: You can also tie bow around base of one handle.

Give Thanks
Table Runner

Materials

- Gray wool scarf (or color of choice)
- Satin ribbon: ⅜" orange, 1¼" olive, ⅜" bright pink, ¼" rust, 1½" teal
- Fusible hem tape
- Gray sewing thread
- Large seed beads in olive tones
- Metal alphabet charms

Tools

- Iron
- Sewing needle
- Scissors

With a wool fabric scarf as the base, make a pretty runner to display a lovely sentiment for your Thanksgiving gathering.

COST: $21.00

TIME: 50 minutes

- See photos for details and placement.

1 Prepare ribbons. Cut two lengths of each ribbon color 1" longer than the width of the scarf. Cut a piece of hem tape for each ribbon, trimming as necessary to fit the width of the ribbon. For wide ribbon pieces, lay two hem tape pieces side by side.

2 Attach ribbons. Arrange the ribbons on one end of the scarf as you like, allowing room for the placement of the alphabet charms. Lay hem tapes under the ribbon nearest the scarf end. Following the manufacturer's directions, iron the ribbon to the scarf, being careful not to iron the ribbon that runs beyond the edge of the scarf. Repeat for the remainder of the ribbons. Arrange ribbons on the other end of the scarf in the same pattern and secure in the same way.

3 Secure ribbon ends. Turn the scarf over and fold the ribbon ends to the back. Iron the ribbons in place.

4 Attach letters. Arrange the alphabet charms on the scarf front to spell, "Give Thanks." Thread needle and knot thread. Sew the charms to the scarf, sewing a seed bead to the top of each charm as an accent.

121

Thanksgiving
Memory Pocket Album

Materials

- 2 pieces of 5½" x 6" terra-cotta mat board (covers)
- 2 sheets of 12" x 12" fall-theme double-sided card stock
- Fall leaves stamp
- 12" x 12" card stock (1 each): gold, rust, terra cotta
- Brown pigment ink pad
- Metal clips
- Clear embossing powder
- 1 yard of ¼" grosgrain ribbon
- Foam dots
- Glue

Tools

- Heat-embossing tool
- Pencil
- Scissors
- Decorative-edge scissors: scallop
- ¼" hole punch

Start a new family tradition this year. Have guests write what they are thankful for on the back of their place cards. Collect the cards and place them into a pocket.

COST: $15.00

TIME: 1½ hours

- Trace and cut out patterns (see page 153).
- See photos for details and placement.

1 Emboss cover. Cut two 5½" x 6" pieces from terra cotta mat board. Press the edges of covers along the stamp pad and dip into embossing powder. Emboss using the heat-embossing tool.

2 Stamp cover panel. Stamp leaf image onto gold card stock using embossing pad. Sprinkle embossing powder over the image, tapping off excess. Emboss using the heat-embossing tool. Cut around the outside of the image using the decorative-edge scissors.

3 Assemble cover. Place the front cover of the book on a flat surface. Lay a 30" length of ribbon horizontally on top of book cover, allowing 8" to extend off the back edge. Use foam dots to adhere the stamped image to the front of the mat board book cover, covering the ribbon. Use a computer or hand print "Thankful Hearts" onto rust card stock. Trim to 1¼" x 3½" rectangle. Glue to front cover of book, covering the ribbon.

1

4 Make pockets. Using double-sided patterned card stock, cut three 6" x 12" pockets. Score along the 12" length at the 5½" and then 10⅝" measurements.
Fold the card stock along the score lines, gluing the narrow flap over the top of the first fold. Glue one end of the pocket closed. Repeat to create additional pockets.

5 Make accordion spine. Cut a 5½" x 11" strip of card stock and score along the 11" length at 1" intervals. Fold the strip back and forth to create an accordion-style book spine. Glue the front edge of the book spine to the inside cover of the book. Glue the bottom edge of pockets to the back edge of each accordion fold. Glue the end of the book spine to the inside of the back cover. Cut a piece of card stock 5½" x 6". Stamp with leaves stamp in same way as cover panel. Glue to front inside cover of the book covering the accordion folded hinge.

6 Make tags. Trace one tag pattern onto gold, rust, and terra-cotta card stock. Cut out. Punch a hole in the top of each tag. Write dates on the front of the tags. Cut three 4" lengths of ribbon. Insert end of one ribbon through a mini clip and through the hole in tag. Overlap ribbon ends and glue together. Repeat for other tags. Close pockets with clips.

7 Make leaves. Trace both leaf patterns onto three colors of card stock and cut out. Make one for each guest. Write guests' names on front of leaves and use as place cards at the dinner table. Invite guests to write a Thanksgiving message on the back of their place card. Collect them after dinner and insert them into pocket. Add a personal message to the front of the pocket and clip it closed until next year.

7

Maple Leaf Painted Tray

Materials

- 9½" square wooden tray
- 11" x 17" white paper (for pattern)
- Light cardboard
- Masking tape
- Oil pencils: dark red/burgundy, orange, copper/brown, green/olive
- Clear matte-finish spray

Tools

- Ruler
- No. 2 pencil
- Straight pins
- Scissors

On a purchased wooden tray, use oil pencils for an open and natural painted look that highlights the wood grain. The "quilt block" design is easy to draw and color. It creates a rich Thanksgiving tone for your table or living room accent.

COST: $15.00
TIME: 1½ hours

- Enlarge and cut out pattern (see page 153).
- See photos for details and placement.

1 Make pattern insert. Use pencil and ruler to make pattern the size of tray following the figure. If size of tray is larger or rectangular, add larger borders. If border is larger than 1", break it up into squares or triangles. Cut pattern paper to size of tray. Center in tray and tape edges.

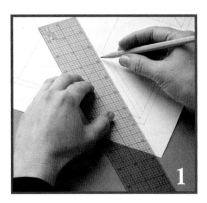

2 Complete design. Pin line intersections on outside of design, plus both ends of the stem of flower pattern. Do this by pressing pins firmly into wood. Remove pattern. Make a straight edge strip from the cardboard 2" wide and ½" shorter than tray size. Note: This will allow you to get into the corners. Connect all lines, using cardboard straight edge. To draw diagonal lines, cut a 1" x 4½" straight edge.

3 Color design. With oil pencils, color the border first. Color with the grain when possible. Color the leaf areas first, working from the top of leaf down, or from one side to the

other. Avoid resting your hand on colored area. Color the stem. Note: Use the cardboard straight edge as a guide when coloring to help keep edges colored evenly.

4 Finish. Spray tray with a matte-finish spray to seal the colors and the wood.

Materials

- 10 feet of 22-gauge wire
- ¾ yard of multi-colored cotton Christmas fabric, 44" wide
- Curly raffia
- ⅛ yard of green cotton print fabric, 44" wide
- 18 silver 20mm jingle bells

Tools

- Wire cutter
- Ruler
- Scissors
- Toothpick
- Glue gun and glue sticks
- Iron

Create a country garland that can be used with your artificial or real Christmas greens to dress up mirrors, picture frames, or chandeliers. And best of all, you determine the "look" and lengths you need.

COST: $25.00

TIME: 1 hour

- See photos for details and placement.

1 Tear rag strips. Cut a 1" long snip 1" wide on the selvage (the finished edge) of the Christmas fabric. Holding the fabric in both hands with the cut in the middle, rip the entire length of fabric for 1 rag strip. Discard the first narrow torn piece. From the torn edge of the fabric, make another 1" wide snip. Rip the fabric in the same way. Rip strips with the remaining fabric. Iron all the rag pieces and pull off any long threads.

2 Cut wire. Use wire cutter to cut a piece of 22-gauge wire 10 feet long. Bend the wire in half. With your fingers, twist the ends of the wires together. Bend them over 1" at a 90-degree angle.

3 Cover wire with strips. Put a bead of hot glue on the end of one strip on the wrong side of the fabric. Quickly place the end of the wire in the hot glue and allow it to cool. Wrap the rag strip around the wire in a spiral fashion, overlapping about half of the previous strip with each turn. To add another strip, wrap it around itself a few times to hold in place and then continue wrapping in a spiral. Note: You can also hot-glue the second rag strip to the first one if you like. To finish covering the wire, cut excess fabric and glue end of strip to wire.

4 Make the bell strips. Tear a 1" wide strip of green fabric. Cut into six 8" lengths. Use a toothpick to push the end of one strip through the top hole of a bell. Position the bell in the middle of the strip. Add another bell on each side of the first one. Make six three-bell strips.

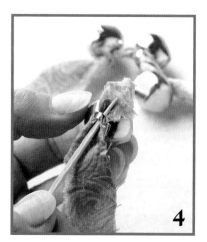

5 Finish. Tie the bells on to the garland 11" apart. Cut off the fabric ends to 1¾" lengths. Tie five strands of curly raffia around each bell strip. Cut off raffia ends to 1½" lengths. Option: Cinnamon sticks can be used in place of the jingle bells.

Christmas Card

Materials

- 5½" x 8½" green card stock
- Red and white paper scraps
- "Merry Christmas" stamp
- Red stamp pad
- 6" twig
- 1 yard of green chenille yarn
- Paper glue
- 8" length of ⅛" red gingham ribbon
- Textured snow
- 5 red snaps

Tools

- Ruler
- Scoring tool
- ⅛" hole punch
- Snap setter
- Pencil
- Paintbrush
- Scissors

You'll have to look twice to tell whether this is a real cedar branch or yarn!

COST: $20.00 for 10 cards

TIME: 2 hours for 10 cards

- See photos for details and placement.

1 Make card. Use ruler and scoring tool to mark a line 4¼" in from 5½" edge. Fold paper in half to measure 4¼" x 5½".

2 Make message. Stamp "Merry Christmas" on white paper. Cut a rectangle around words, leaving a ¼" border. Glue on red paper. Cut around edges, leaving a ⅛" border. Glue to lower right corner of card.

3 Make branch. Cut twig to fit across card. Cut short lengths of yarn and glue to twig to look like a cedar branch.

4 Attach branch. Punch two holes in top right corner of card where twig will lie. Thread ribbon through holes. Glue branch to card. Tie ribbon in a bow around twig. Cut ends at a slant.

5 Finish. Apply snow to branches. Let dry. Make five small dots with a pencil where you want to place a "berry." Set a red snap at each dot.

Glistening Berry Wreath

Materials

- 12" floral wire wreath frame
- 6 white berry holiday picks
- 6 red berry holiday picks
- 36" of 2½" white wire-edged ribbon
- 2½ yards of 2½" red wire-edged ribbon
- Floral tape
- 26" of 22-gauge wire

Tools

- Needle-nose pliers
- Glue gun and glue sticks
- Scissors

Create an elegant holiday wreath with just a little twisting, tying, and gluing.

COST: Under $20.00

TIME: 1 hour

- See photos for details and placement.

1 Prepare wire frame. Use pliers to open the wires holding the outer wire circle in place. Remove the outer wire circle. Use the pliers to cut off the wires that held the outer wire circle.

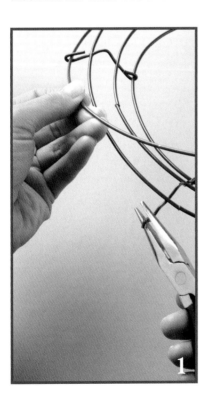

2 Attach berry pick. Place a white berry pick with the stem lying on the outside wire of frame. Bend it slightly to match the curve of the frame. Wind a 5" piece of floral tape around the stem of the pick in a spiral fashion, pulling on it a little as you wind it. At the bottom of the stem, pinch the tape and stem together.

3 Attach remaining picks. Place a red berry pick close to the white one with the stem lying on the middle wire of frame. Attach it to the frame in same way as first pick. Alternate white and red berry picks around the frame, leaving a 4½" space at bottom for the bow. Position the leaves and berries so that the frame is not showing.

4 Make red bow. Cut six pieces of red ribbon 9" long. Fold each ribbon in half and glue the ends together. Cut a 6" length of wire. Gather three of the glued ribbon loops together and tightly wrap the ends of the ribbons with the wire. Twist the wire tightly with the pliers. Trim the wire to ½" long. Wire three more ribbon loops together in the same way. Cut an 8" length of wire. Place the two ribbon groups together and wrap the wire around them tightly. Do not cut wire ends.

133

Molded Clay
Christmas Ornament

Materials

- 2½" craft foam ball
- Air-dry modeling compound
- Fresh leaf
- Ivory beads: six round, one oval, one heart-shaped
- 5 head pins
- 3 eye pins
- 8" of clear fishing line
- Glue

Tools

- Rolling pin
- Holly leaf cookie cutter
- Round-nose pliers
- Scissors

Create one-of-a-kind ornaments for family and friends. Simple techniques combine air-dry modeling compound with a foam ball and a few beads. You're done!

COST: $10.00

TIME: 1½ hours

- See photos for details and placement.

1 Cover foam ball. Roll a 3" ball of modeling compound to ⅛" thickness. Turn the compound many times to prevent sticking. Center the foam ball in center of compound and wrap the compound around the ball. Press the compound around the surface of the ball, eliminating air bubbles. Use scissors to trim any excess compound. Roll the ball on a flat surface to eliminate fingerprints. Set aside.

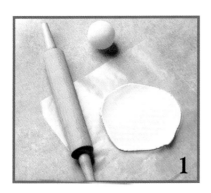

2 Make leaves. Roll a second 3" ball of compound to ⅛" thickness. Use the cookie cutter to cut out 12 leaves. Press the back of a fresh leaf into the shaped compound leaf to create veining and natural indentations. Gently pinch the edges and shape the leaf into a realistic shape.

3 Attach leaves. Add a drop of glue to the back of the leaf and gently press into place at the top of the ball. Repeat with other leaves, overlapping them.

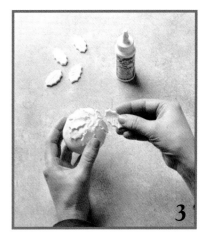

4 Add beads. Insert an eye pin into a round bead and push pin into the top center of the ball. Remove, apply a drop of glue, and replace. Apply a drop of glue to the end of a second eye pin and push it into the bottom center of the ball. Insert third eye pin into one oval bead and one heart-shaped bead. Cut end of eye pin to ¼" length. Use pliers to form wire into a ring. Attach it to the bottom eye pin and close wire ring.

5 Finish. Insert one head pin into one round bead, five times. Dip ends of head pins into glue and press into center of poinsettia flower at the top of the ball. For hanger, insert an 8" length of fishing line through eye pin at the top of ball. Tie ends together in an overhand knot.

135

Ice Skate Stockings

Materials

- Vinyl: white, silver
- Medium-weight cardboard
- Ten ¾" gold (or silver) grommets
- One white eyelet
- 2 yards of 1" pink sheer ribbon
- 10" of pink ¼" ribbon
- Sewing thread: silver, pink

Tools

- Grommet setter, pad and hammer
- Eyelet setter
- Tracing paper
- Pencil
- Sewing machine
- Scissors

This symbol of the season can hang up long after St. Nick's visit. Use the fun footwear to hold boughs of evergreen until winter's end.

COST: $14.00

TIME: 2 hours

- Enlarge and cut out patterns (see page 154).
- See photos for details and placement.
- Sew scant ¼" seam allowances.

1 Cut patterns. Use patterns to cut a Skate Front and a Skate Back from white vinyl. Cut one Skate Blade from silver vinyl, placing the bottom edge on fold. Cut one Blade Insert from cardboard. Mark the grommet placements on Skate Front as indicated on pattern.

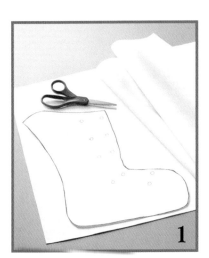

2 Attach grommets. Cut a tiny slit at each grommet marking. Use scissors to cut out a pea-size circle around each slit. Push a grommet through the hole. Follow the manufacturer's directions for securing grommets.

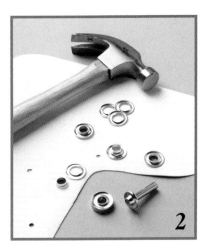

3 Sew blade. Place blade insert into the silver blade piece. With the cardboard sandwiched between the vinyl, stitch all of the way around the blade shape with silver thread.

4 Sew details. Use machine and pink thread to sew details on skate fronts: as indicated on pattern. Note: Use decorative machine stitches if you like.

5 Assemble skate. Place the skate front and back together with edges even. Insert the folded blade piece at bottom of skate. Sew one continuous seam with pink thread having the blade sandwiched in between. Sew down one side, across bottom, and up other side. Backstitch and clip threads. Lace the skates with 1" ribbon, tying the ends into a bow. Cut ends at a slant.

6 Make hanger. For eyelet, punch a hole through the top left corner of the skate. Push an eyelet in the hole. Follow the manufacturer's directions for securing eyelet. Insert ¼" ribbon through the hole. Tie ends in an overhand knot.

Mat Board Card Box

Materials

- 12" x 24" red mat board
- Christmas rubber stamps
- Ink pads: green, red, black
- 21" of ¾" green ribbon
- 1¼" metal buckle charm
- 4" of ¾" magnet strip
- Double-sided tape
- Alphabet foam stamps

Tools

- Pencil
- Cork-backed ruler
- Craft knife
- Stencil brush
- Scissors

A box like this filled with personalized cards for family and friends is sure to be a hit with everyone on your list!

COST: $15.00

TIME: 1½ hours

- The colored side of mat board is the right side.
- See photos for details and placement.
- Enlarge and trace patterns (see page 153).

1 Cut and score pieces. For Inside Box, cut a 4½" x 13" piece of mat board. Mark scoring lines 3" and 3½" in on both ends of board. Score on the right side. For Outside Cover, cut a 6" x 10" piece of mat board. Mark scoring lines 2¼" and 2¾" in on both ends of board. Score on right side.

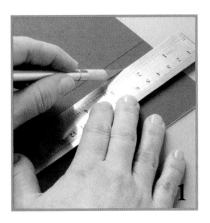

2 Stamp mat board. Stamp "Merry Merry" and "Christmas" in black ink on Outside Cover flap as indicated on pattern. Stamp Christmas images with green ink on the white side of both pieces of mat board. With stencil brush, dab red ink around edges of Outside Cover to shade it.

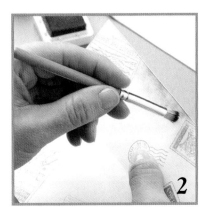

3 Attach ribbon. Run a line of double-sided tape on back of ribbon. Position one end of the ribbon on the center of the wrong side of the "Christmas" flap. Wrap ribbon around box to other flap.

4 Attach magnets. Cut two pieces of magnet to fit the back of the metal charm. Adhere one magnet on top of the ribbon end on the "Christmas" flap. Insert ribbon through the buckle charm and adhere other magnet to the ribbon on back of charm.

5 Finish. Cut a 6" length of ribbon. Tie it in a knot around the ribbon just below the charm. Cut ends at a slant. Position Inside Box on bottom and Outside Cover on top, forming a cross. Adhere two pieces to each other with double-sided tape.

Scoring Tips

Practice before working on project. The goal is to cut a little more than halfway through the board but do not cut all the way through it. Measure and mark scoring lines in pencil. Line up metal ruler on line. Press craft knife down firmly and go over scoring line two or three times. If you have not scored deeply enough it will be difficult to bend. Then take your knife and go over your line again. If you score too deeply and cut through the board, patch it with clear bandage tape from the inside before assembling.

Tin Lid Wreath

Materials

- *Metal tin lids: 8", 5½", 4"*
- *56" length of 2½" red plaid wire-edged ribbon*
- *Wood scrap*
- *Nail*
- *3 yards of medium-weight wire*
- *Large silver jingle bell*

Tools

- *Hammer*
- *Wire cutter*

Coordinating lids appear as an oversized ornament. With so many tins available, you'll have fun finding just the right ones to match your decor.

COST: $13.00

TIME: 1¼ hours

- See photos for details and placement.
- Let paint dry thoroughly after each application.

1 Punch holes. Use a scrap piece of wood to protect work surface. With hammer and a nail, punch holes at the top center and bottom center of each tin lid rim. Hold the lid upright and hammer nail through the rim of lid.

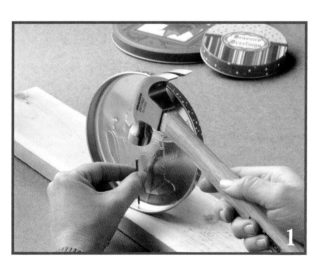

3 Make hanger. Make a hanging loop with wire and twist wire ends to secure them inside the top lid. Wrap ribbon around the wire and tie in a bow. Cut ends at a slant.

2 Wire lids together. Cut a 3-yard length of wire and fold it in half. Insert wire through top of bell and slide it to the center. With wire ends together, insert wire through holes in lids beginning with the smallest bottom one and then each larger one. Pull wire tight so there is no space between lids.

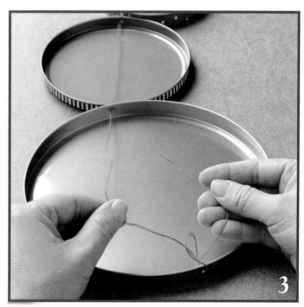

141

Stuffed Mittens

Materials

- 14" x 20" wool fabric: red, tan
- Small amount of white wool roving
- 1 skein brown embroidery floss
- 20" of ⅜" red grosgrain ribbon
- ¾" white star button
- White sewing thread
- 6" x 8" craft foam, 4" thick
- Paper

Tools

- 36-gauge felting needle
- Sewing needle
- Embroidery needle
- Pencil
- Clear ruler
- Straight pins
- Scissors

Create this handmade pair of mittens and use them in place of hanging stockings. They are easy to place over a chair back, bedpost, or banister. The unique design feature of needle felting is easy to learn and any easy design, including an initial, works well.

COST: $4.00

TIME: 1⅛ hours

- Enlarge mitten pattern to 9½" length and cut out two (see page 156).
- See photos for details and placement.
- Felting needles are very sharp. Use with care.

1 Cut out patterns. Label one pattern Mitten Back. Cut the other pattern apart diagonally as indicated on pattern. Label pieces Top Mitten Front and Bottom Mitten Front. Add a ½" seam allowance along the diagonal cut of the Bottom Mitten Front. Place wool fabric with right sides together. Cut two Mitten Backs, and two bottom Mitten Front pieces from red fabric. Cut two top Mitten Front pieces from tan fabric. Mark the right side of the fabric pieces with a pin.

2 Practice needle felting. Place a scrap piece of wool fabric over the foam. Place roving over fabric, pulling gently into line. With felting needle, poke up and down many times. Try not to cut roving. Add more roving or pull for a thinner look.

3 Needle-felt stars. After practicing, place roving on mitten bottom front. Adhere about 2" of roving for the first side of the star, poking fast and often. You can always go back and poke more. Turn star point and continue making the five sides of the star. It is fine to have unbalanced sides to the star. When done, pull fabric piece off the foam.

4 Stitch X's. Place top front and bottom front together, overlapping ½" along diagonal. Use four strands of embroidery floss to stitch large X's across the seam, catching both fabrics at the top of stitches. Irregular stitches are fine.

5 Blanket stitch. Pin front and back of mitten wrong sides together. Starting at top of mitten, use six strands of embroidery floss to stitch around mitten in blanket stitch. Place stitches about ½" apart and ⅜" deep. Irregular stitches are fine.

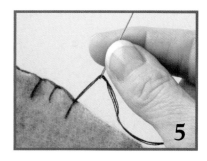

6 Make hanger. Cut a 20" length of ribbon. Place one end at top corner of one mitten between the front and back and stitch in place. Add button over stitching. Attach other end of ribbon to other mitten in same way.

143

Stitches

Stitch Guide

Blanket Stitch:
Crazy for Clovers Felt
Table Mat, page 28
Felt Egg Cozies, page 46

Running Stitch:
Crazy for Clovers Felt
Table Mat, page 28
Felt Egg Cozies, page 46
Berried Bookmarks, page 58

Crow-Stitch:
Wall Hanging Quilt, page 38

Back Stitch:
Wall Hanging Quilt, page 38

French Knot:
Wall Hanging Quilt, page 38
Berried Bookmarks, page 58

3 Chain Stitch:
Felt Egg Cozies, page 46

Long Stitch:
Berried Bookmarks, page 58

Zig Zag Stitch:
Bright Appliquéd
Table Runner, page 50

Blanket Stitch
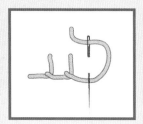

Back Stitch

Running Stitch

Long Stitch

Crow-Stitch
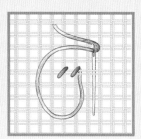

French Knot

3 Chain Stitch

Zig Zag Stitch
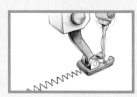

Confetti Place Mats: Page 6

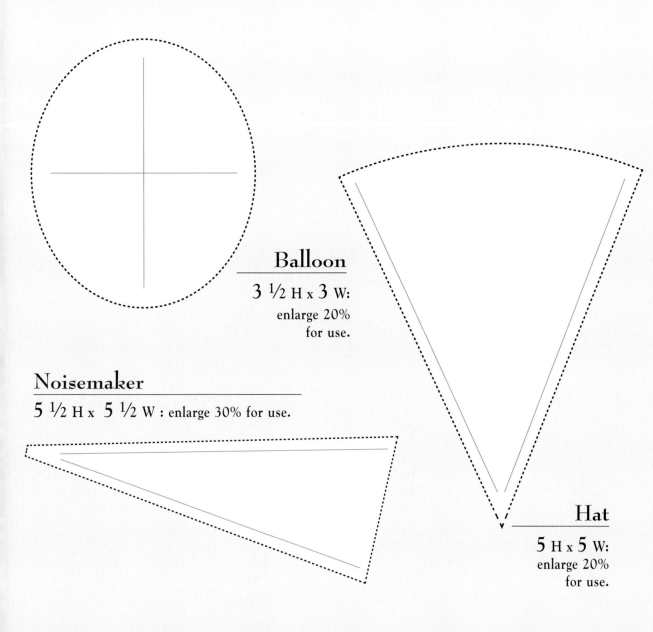

Balloon

3 ½ H x **3** W:
enlarge 20%
for use.

Noisemaker

5 ½ H x **5 ½** W : enlarge 30% for use.

Hat

5 H x **5** W:
enlarge 20%
for use.

New Years

Embellished Place Mat and Napkin, Page 14

Swirl
Pattern

enlarge 40%
for use.

Valentine's Day & St. Patrick's Day

Valentine's Day, **Beaded Box,** Page 24

Heart Pattern
sized at 100%

Clover Pattern
enlarge 50% for use.

St. Patrick's Day,
Crazy for Clovers Felt Table Mat, Page 28

Easter &
Cinco de Mayo

Easter, **Felt Egg Cozies,** Page 46

Egg Cozy
Pattern

enlarge 30% for use.

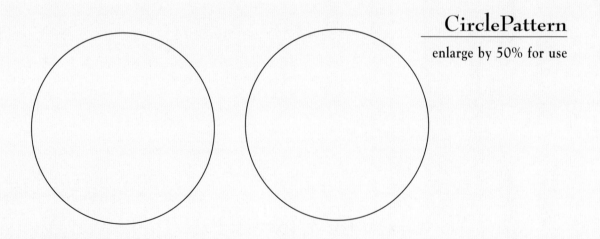

Cinco de Mayo, **Bright Appliquéd Table Runner,** Page 50

CirclePattern

enlarge by 50% for use

Mother's Day & Memorial Day

Mother's Day, Gardening Apron, Page 60

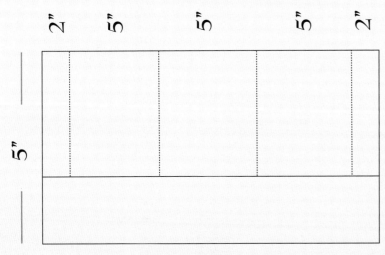

2" 5" 5" 5" 2"

5"

8"

19"

Apron Pattern

enlarge 60% for use

Memorial Day

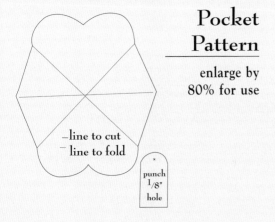

– line to cut
– line to fold

punch
1/8"
hole

Pocket Pattern

enlarge by 80% for use

Cone Pattern

enlarge by 75% for use

Memorial Day Pockets,

Page 66

Hanging Cones with Floral,

Page 70

Father's Day &
4th of July

Father's Day

Fish BBQ Apron, Page 72

Fish Pattern

enlarge by 50% for use

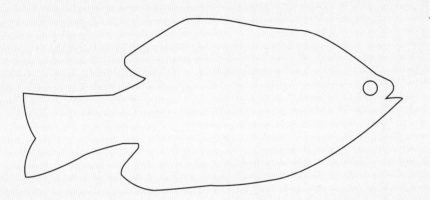

4th of July, Wood Patriotic Flag, Page 80

Flag Pattern

enlarge by 60% for use

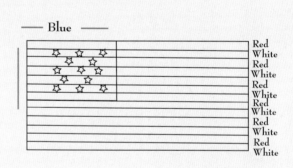

Halloween

Felt Trick-or-Treat Bag,
Page 92

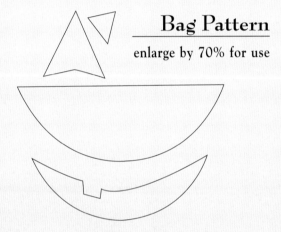

Bag Pattern
enlarge by 70% for use

Skeleton Topiary,
Page 106

Face Pattern
pattern at 100%

Draped Candelabra,
Page 96

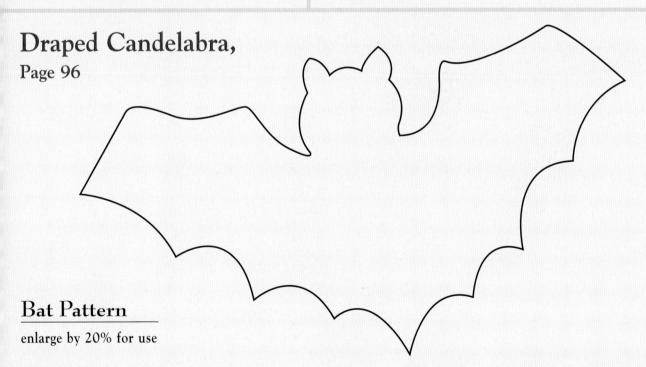

Bat Pattern
enlarge by 20% for use

151

Halloween

Boo'tiful Crocheted Treat Bag, Page 98

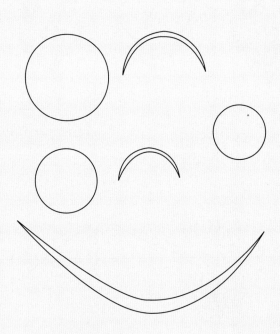

Bag Pattern

enlarge by 60% for use

Felt Wallhanging, Page 110

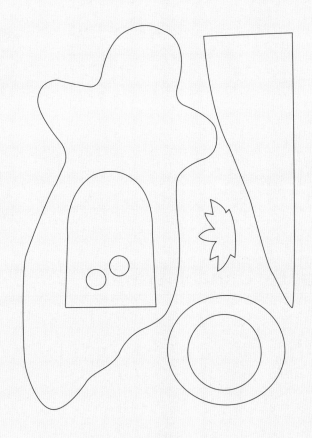

Felt Pattern

enlarge by 65% for use

Thanksgiving

Embellished Basket,
Page 118

Leaf Pattern
enlarge by 30% for use

Memory Pocket Album,
Page 122

Leaf Pattern
enlarge by 50% for use

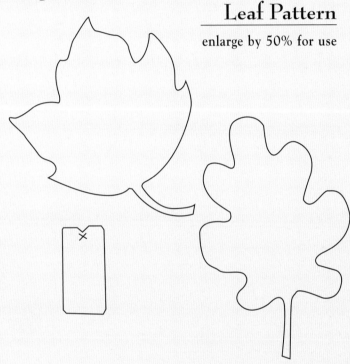

Maple Leaf Painted Tray,
Page 126

Leaf Pattern
enlarge by 50% for use

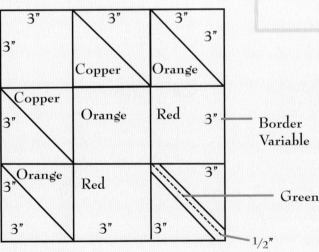

Painted Wood Candlesticks,
Page 116

Leaf Pattern
pattern at 100%

Christmas

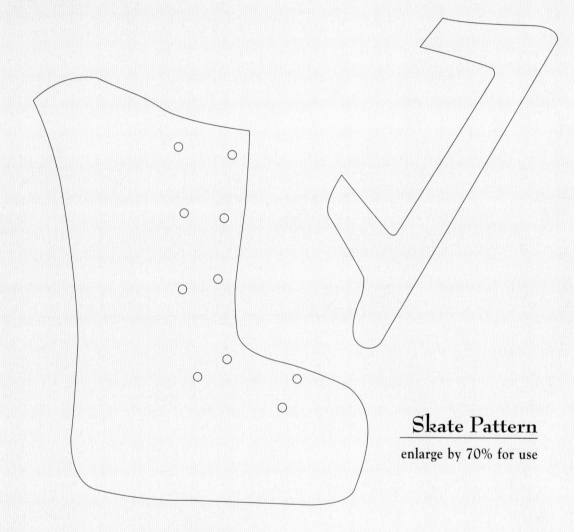

Ice Skate Stockings,
Page 136

Skate Pattern
enlarge by 70% for use

Mat Board Card Box, Page 138

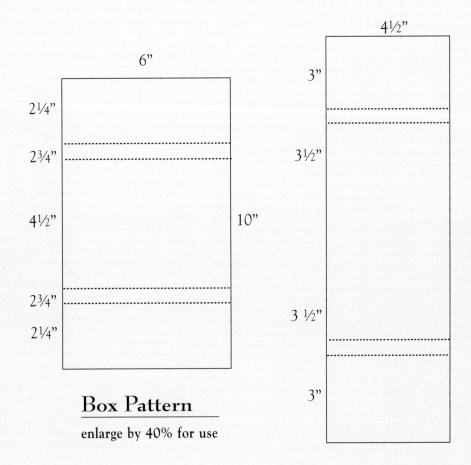

6"

2¼"

2¾"

4½"

10"

2¾"

2¼"

Box Pattern

enlarge by 40% for use

4½"

3"

3½"

3 ½"

3"

Christmas

Stuffed Mittens,
Page 142

**Mitten
Pattern**

enlarge by
40% for use

Index